The World of the ADVENTIST TEENAGER

The World of the ADVENTIST TEENAGER

ROGER L. DUDLEY, Ed.D.

Director of the Institute of Church Ministry
Professor of Christian Ministry
Seventh-day Adventist Theological Seminary
Andrews University

and

JANET LEIGH KANGAS, Ph.D.

Missions Editor
Church Ministries Department
General Conference of Seventh-day Adventists

REVIEW AND HERALD® PUBLISHING ASSOCIATION
WASHINGTON, DC 20039-0555
HAGERSTOWN, MD 21740

This book was
Edited by Richard W. Coffen
Designed by Bill Kirstein

PRINTED IN U.S.A.

95 94 93 92 91 90 10 9 8 7 6 5 4 3 2 1

R&H Cataloging Service
Dudley, Roger L
The world of the Adventist teenager, by Roger L. Dudley and Janet Leigh Kangas.

1. Youth—Religious life. 2. Religious surveys—Seventh-day Adventists. 3. Seventh-day Adventists—Religious life. 4. Seventh-day Adventists—Youth—Religious life. I. Kangas, Janet Leigh, 1943- joint author. II. Title.

301.452867

ISBN 0-8280-0562-1

Acknowledgments

Unless otherwise credited, all Scriptural passages are from the *Holy Bible, New International Version*. Copyright © 1973, 1978, International Bible Society. Used by permission of Zondervan Bible Publishers.

Contents

Chapter

One — Hemorrhage in the Church / 9

Two — There's No Place Like Home / 17

Three — Families That Pray Together . . . / 29

Four — Love/Hate the Church / 38

Five — This Is the Way We Go to Church / 47

Six — Skewered on Standards / 54

Seven — Young Disciples / 65

Eight — A Multi-million Dollar Enterprise / 76

Nine — Fallout From the Rat Race / 88

Ten — Call Person to Person / 98

Eleven — One-on-One With God / 108

Twelve — One Year Later / 120

Afterword / 132

Appendix — Methodology of the Study / 138

CHAPTER 1

Hemorrhage in the Church

I would like to say that I hate my dumb religion and everything about it. I do not understand God, and if I had to choose between my becoming a pig farmer or staying an Adventist, my answer most undoubtedly would be: a pig farmer. I will never fully commit my life to God, and it would take a hell of a miracle to make me believe in Him fully, trust Him, and love Him. DO NOT PRAY FOR ME. DO NOT!"

Would you say this young woman is hostile toward religion? At risk for dropping out of the church? Her write-in comments come from our ongoing study of more than 1,500 Seventh-day Adventist teenagers. Is she typical? How many more are like her?

Of course, the problem is not limited to the Adventist church. David Roozen reported on an ecumenical study of church disengagement and re-entry. Based on the 1978 Gallup survey of unchurched Americans, it revealed that nearly 46 percent of Americans drop out of church participation at some time in their lives. The peak dropout rate occurs during the teenage years.

Probable causes for the dropout rate listed by people in this age group were the lessening of parental influence as peer pressure and the emancipation process gained influence, plus the feeling that the church had little to offer that was relevant or interesting.[1]

The issue is far from trivial. Potentially, any church is but one generation from extinction and, therefore, must lay serious plans to transmit its religious heritage. Great ideals do not live on simply because they are great or true. They survive only as they are enshrined in the hearts of the children. The torch must not fall.[2]

One of our young male respondents wrote: "I think that the church is starting to decline because it is losing its young people. They say that in the last days it's the children who will lead the world. Well, the church better do something before all the children leave."

But before we conclude that the game is over and the war is lost—before we retreat and confine our activities to making the remaining saints comfortable during their declining years—let's look at the other side. We found teenagers who love their religion and their church. Enjoy these comments by three different adolescents.

"The feelings I have when I think of my religion are something more than words can describe. They are feelings of joy, happiness, adventure, and learning—all at the same time."

"Sometimes I feel like not sleeping or not eating so I can learn more about the greatest being in the universe, God."

"I feel happy about my religion because I know it is the right one. The people are united and are like a big family. I also know and have seen Jesus and the Holy Spirit work. It is enough to bring tears to my eyes."

Two viewpoints. Which one is closer to reality? And what makes the difference? Those questions are what this book is all about. Let's search together for some answers.

The Big Question

The telephone rings. The minister at the other end has a question. "I'm going to preach about saving our youth this Sabbath. Somewhere I've heard that 75 percent of them leave the church. Can you give me the correct figure?"

This question, or some variant, is undoubtedly the one that

has been posed most often to the staff at the Institute of Church Ministry over the years. The answer? Nobody really knows. Many of us look at our local spheres of responsibility and form hunches. Some area studies have been done. But we simply have not compiled the data that would allow conclusions on a division-wide basis. And the reason is clear: Such data are extremely difficult and expensive to come by.

In the first place, there is no master list (in most cases not even local lists) of young people who have left the church. And even if there were, it would be nearly impossible to secure current mailing addresses. People who drop out tend to disappear, and young adults usually establish a different residence after leaving adolescence. Also former members are often bitter and not likely to respond in any great proportion to a mail survey from the church.

Of course, we want to know not only how many have dropped out but *why* they have left so that we can take corrective action. But even if we could interview these former members, they would (and could) probably give us only the precipitating causes—those things that were high in their consciousness at the moment. They would not be able to uncover the home, school, and church influences of their early years that had moved them toward loyal church participation or disappointed departure.

Not that we know nothing at all. Some studies on Adventists have illuminated the general pathway. Charles Martin conducted one of the earliest—in 1963. He surveyed students in four Midwestern Adventist academies. He found that 78 percent of the youth went to church because they really wanted to, but only 55.5 percent agreed that "the doctrines are clear to me and I believe them." Nearly 22 percent believed that the church had too many restrictions.[3]

Ten years later Stanley Hardt administered the Martin questionnaire in two other academies. He wanted to find out if attitudes had changed during this period of time. Hardt found a number of significant shifts—in every case in a more negative direction regarding religion.[4]

Joel Noble, in 1971, studied twelfth-grade students in nine academies in the Pacific Northwest. He found that his subjects' belief of church doctrines was less than their knowledge of them, and their practice of Adventist principles was less than their professed belief in them. Also, students in these schools tended to be more critical of the religious instruction than of other aspects of the academic program.[5]

In 1973, Ila Zbaraschuk reported on interviews with an unspecified number of young people who had already withdrawn from church membership. She estimated that 50 percent of Adventist adolescents actually sever their church connections. Among reasons given for leaving were: (1) church membership without personal conversion, (2) impersonal, not-caring attitude on the part of older members, (3) phony-appearing lives of adult members, (4) no sense of relevance to needs, (5) religion didn't make a difference in one's own life and didn't want to be a hypocrite, (6) absence of thinking for oneself, (7) misplaced emphasis with nonessentials too important, (8) academy disciplinary methods, (9) preoccupation with organization on part of leaders, and (10) quality of sermons.[6]

In a small 1977 study, Grey Banta interviewed 23 Adventists and 14 former Adventists from California. He wanted to know why members leave the church. The former members reported being influenced to separate by the following factors (listed in descending order of importance): neglect of daily worship, church leaders, loss of interest in Bible study, negative experiences in church school and academy, and financial expense. The people who most influenced them to leave were academy principals, academy teachers, conference leaders, pastors, and academy deans.[7]

Also in 1977 Louis Nielsen interviewed 150 former Adventists in Michigan (not necessarily youth). He found the following overlapping factors offered for their separation: avoidance of hypocrisy (more than 50 percent), loss of interest (50 percent), premature baptism (more than 25 percent), got nothing out of going to church (25 percent), hurt feelings (nearly 25 percent), no close friends in the church (nearly 25 percent), and followed spouse's example (nearly 15 percent).[8]

One of the few national studies ever conducted of Adventist youth was reported by the senior author in 1978. It concluded that about 16 percent of academy students could be considered alienated from religion in general and that an additional 36 percent had hostile feelings toward certain areas of religion though they were generally positive. Thus more than 50 percent might be described as either generally or selectively put off by the church and its values.[9]

A more recent study by Warren Minder in four Midwestern states reported that most youth who attend the Adventist school system all the way through remain in the church.[10]

If after scanning this review of Adventist research, you are thinking, *That's all very helpful, but I still don't know what percentage of our youth are leaving the church on a division-wide basis or what factors, for sure, make the difference between who stays and who goes*, you are right. We don't know either! But we are on the way toward finding out. Let us share our search with you.

New Ears for Teenage Concerns

The crucial nature of the issue demanded a new plan. The North American Division asked the Institute of Church Ministry (ICM) at Andrews University to tackle the task. We proposed a ten-year longitudinal study. The plan called for us to survey a large representative sample of teenagers who were already in the church. Comprehensive information would be gathered, which would serve as a base with which to compare later events. Then each year, for the next nine years, we would collect smaller sets of information. Hopefully, the continuing relationship developed with each subject would encourage him/her to respond to the yearly questionnaire. And, of course, it would be easier to secure forwarding addresses with only one-year gaps between contacts.

By the time the young adults reached their mid-twenties, most would have made their decisions relative to Christ and the church. We could then compare their present situations with the information gathered through the years to determine what factors predict retention, disaffiliation, denominational service, et cetera.

The first year of the study would be the most difficult since it would involve building the address list and collecting all the base data. Janet Kangas joined ICM to direct this project for her Ph.D. dissertation in Religious Education. The research costs were borne by the North American Division. Two departments were especially enlisted—the Department of Education and the Church Ministries Department.

While the full benefits of this research will not be realized for some years, the first phase has now been completed and has supplied rich material for our understanding of the Adventist teenager. For those who would like more information concerning the methodology of the study, a more complete description has been included in the appendix.

So we will not be able to tell you in this book the percentage of our youth who are leaving—the extent of the hemorrhage in the church. But as the years go by we will keep careful track of what happens to each of our teenagers. We have more than 1,500, all 15 or 16 years old to start with, and all baptized members. Since they have come from churches scientifically selected to represent the entire North American Division, we can have confidence that what happens to them will serve as a sound estimate of the destiny of all our youth in North America.

Neither can we tell you the major factors that predict retention or dropout. This information will result from years of comparing the base and subsequent data with the actual outcome in each particular case. Ten years down the line we will have a picture of the dynamics of adolescence and young adulthood never before seen in the Adventist church and rarely in any other.

So why this book now? Because in collecting the base data

we learned so much about the backgrounds, attitudes, and behaviors of our teenagers that would be valuable to parents, pastors, teachers, and church leaders that we felt compelled to share what we have learned.

We gathered responses to 147 questions. They deal with subjects like baptism, spiritual status of parents, marital status of the home, years of Adventist versus public education, educational and vocational plans, participation in church activities, relationships with people, gaining independence, types of discipline experienced, spiritual influences on life, role models, competition, church standards, attitudes toward Adventists and Adventism, spiritual self-assessment, religious instruction, and devotional practices.

In addition to quantitative, forced-choice questions, young people wrote completions to the following five open-ended statements:

1. The feelings I have when I think of my religion are:
2. The reasons I feel the way I do about my religion are:
3. The first thing I would like to change about my religion is:
4. The most important thing in life to me is:
5. Is there anything else you would like to tell us about yourself?

A rich mine of information indeed! In the succeeding chapters we will open this mine to you, setting it forth in a series of themes. Of special interest are the responses to items like "I intend to remain an Adventist when I am on my own," "I'm happy with my religion," and "I can't imagine I will ever belong to another denomination than Seventh-day Adventism." For if we cannot yet know what the teenagers will actually *do*, we can know what they now *think they will do*. And that knowledge may point us in directions that will save some who otherwise would slip away.

References

[1] David A. Roozen, "Church Dropouts: Changing Patterns of Disengagement and Re-entry," *Review of Religious Research* 21 (Supplement 1980): pp. 427-450.

[2] See Roger L. Dudley, *Passing on the Torch: How to Pass Your Spiritual Values on to Your Children and Teens* (Hagerstown, MD: Review and Herald Publishing Association, 1986).

[3] Charles D. Martin, "Moral and Religious Problems and Attitudes as Expressed by Students in Four Seventh-day Adventist Academies" (M.A. thesis, Andrews University, 1963).

[4] Stanley G. Hardt, "A Comparative Study of the Expressed Moral and Religious Attitudes of Students in Two Adventist Academies to the Expressed Moral and Religious Attitudes of Students in Charles Martin's 1963 Study" (M.A. thesis, Andrews University, 1963)

[5] Joel N. Noble, "Certain Religious and Educational Attitudes of Senior High School Students in Seventh-day Adventist Schools in the Pacific Northwest" (Ph.D. dissertation, University of Oregon, 1971).

[6] Ila Zbaraschuk, "Why Young Adventists Leave the Church," *Insight*, September 11, 1973, pp. 10-14.

[7] Grey Banta, "A Study of Why Seventh-day Adventists Who Attend Seventh-day Adventist Schools Separate From Their Church" (M.A. thesis, Loma Linda University, 1977).

[8] Louis C. Nielsen, "Disassociation: An Investigation Into the Contributing Factors of Backsliding and Separation From the Seventh-day Adventist Church" (D.Min. project, Andrews University, 1977).

[9] Roger L. Dudley, *Why Teenagers Reject Religion and What To Do About It* (Washington, D.C.: Review and Herald Publishing Association, 1978), p. 21.

[10] Warren E. Minder, "A Study of the Relationship between Church-sponsored K-12 Education and Church Membership in the Seventh-day Adventist Church" (Ed.D. dissertation, Western Michigan University, 1985).

CHAPTER 2

There's No Place Like Home

When asked to complete the sentence: "The most important thing in life to me is __________," the *second-highest* response given by the teenagers was "family"—exceeded only by "God." Note how well this corresponds to the following counsel to the church.

"The work of parents underlies every other. Society is composed of families, and is what the heads of families make it. . . . the heart of the community, of the church, and of the nation, is the household. The well-being of society, the success of the church, the prosperity of the nation, depend upon home influences."[1]

If home influences are so vital, they should be an important determinant as to which youth eventually drop out of the church and which stay with it. Therefore, on our base questionnaire we asked a number of questions about the kind of family in which the teenager grew up: the church membership and church attendance of both parents, their marital status, the structure of the home, closeness between youth and parents, discipline, role modeling, and family worship. Eventually, it will be possible to correlate these items with retention or disaffiliation and thus discover the kind of home most likely to produce young people who are committed to Christ and His church.

Of course, that day is several years down the road. But, even now, the information may help us better understand the Adventist home. So in this chapter we give a description of our family variables with the exception of family worship, for which we have reserved a separate chapter.

Family Research

First, let's look at a few points from past research on the influence of the home.

As far back as 1961, Putney and Middleton studied the religious convictions of more than a thousand college students and their parents. They found that young people are most likely to accept a religious ideology if both parents hold it jointly.[2]

A few years later Aldous and Hill reported on a study of 88 families over three generations. They discovered that the family is the most powerful of all agencies studied in determining the church affiliation of succeeding generations.[3]

Several studies from the 1970s are of importance. McCready investigated the passing of patterns of devotional behavior from one generation to another among American Catholics. He found that parental influence outweighs any social class effects.[4]

Johnson reported that religious commitment among young people was related to a warm, supportive family. It highly correlated with religious influences in the home. Students tended to report that their parents were generally similar to themselves in religious commitment, and religious students tended to perceive their families as warmer, happier, and more accepting than non-religious students did.[5]

Strommen discovered a close link between the beliefs of parents and their children in his widespread, cross-denominational research. He concluded that the family is the most significant agent in the process of religious education.[6]

Treston, Whiteman, and Florent agreed that basic adolescent value attitudes have their grounding in the home rather than in such institutions such as the church or the school. Additionally, any counterbalancing effects of these external institutions are relatively small in the face of parental influence and home background.[7]

In a more recent study, Nelsen surveyed 2,774 pre-adolescents. He found that parental religiosity significantly predicted the religiosity of the youth. Those parents who attended church more frequently and communicated the impression that religion was important in their lives tended to have children with strong religious values.[8]

So home, family, and parents have proved to be the difference in holding youth to Christ and the church. But what is the state of the Adventist family? To answer this we turn now to our large and representative sample.

Family Commitment to the Church

Of our 1,511 teenagers, 43 percent were male and 57 percent were female—figures very close to the composition of the general Adventist membership in North America. While all the adolescents were baptized members of the Adventist church (a requirement for inclusion in the sample), not all their parents were. About 68 percent of the fathers and 91 percent of the mothers were members at the time of the survey.

The majority of fathers (55 percent) had joined the church before the teenagers were born, but 18 percent had joined during the pre-teen years and 4 percent during the teen years of the sample, whereas 23 percent had never been members. For mothers, 64 percent had joined before the teenagers were born, 26 percent during the pre-teen years, and 6 percent during the teen years of the sample, and only 4 percent had never been members.

Of course, membership is one thing, but participation may be quite another. So we asked our young people how often their parents attended church. Here's what they said:

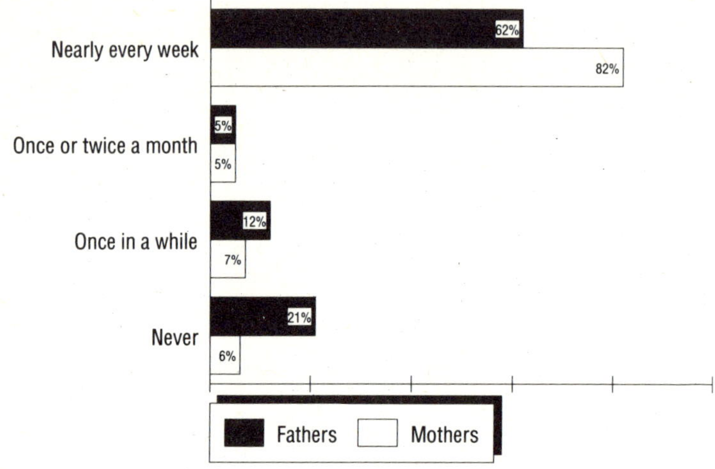

For the fathers, the 62 percent who attended church nearly every week is not too bad since only 68 percent were members. Incidentally, 88 percent of the young people said they attend church nearly every week. Only 2 percent said they never attend. So the youth were doing somewhat better than their parents. Of course, we do not know the extent to which such participation is voluntary.

Since 23 percent more mothers than fathers were Adventist members at the time of the study, it is obvious that the sample represents a number of spiritually divided homes. Actually, about 65 percent of our teenagers came from homes where both parents were Adventists. In the other 35 percent one or both parents were nonmembers.

Does this make a difference in youth attitudes? We contrasted the two groups on seven key items concerning religious attitudes and future intentions. Table 2-1 shows the results.

In every case, those who came from religiously intact homes were more positive toward religion and the church. Happiness with religion and intention to remain Adventists both showed a

TABLE 2-1

Comparison of Attitudes Between TEENAGERS FROM HOMES WHERE BOTH PARENTS ARE SDA AND HOMES WHERE THEY ARE NOT

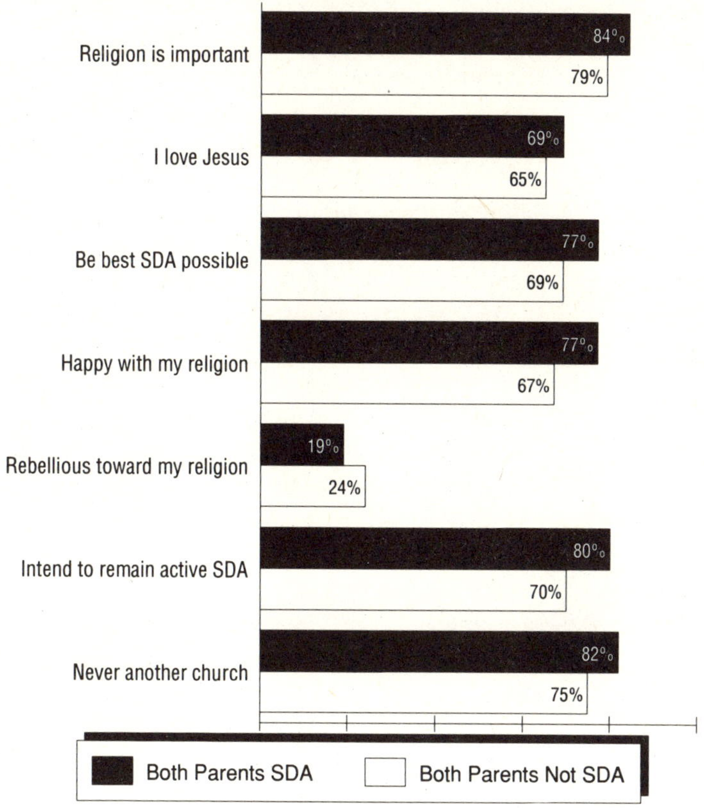

ten-point difference. Also those from united homes were significantly more likely to desire to marry Adventists than the others were. When both parents teach the same values, the united religious influence is stronger than if the teenagers are weighing the value systems of each parent separately.

Family Structure

"I come from a family that is broken up," wrote one young person who had both half- and step-siblings. "I think it is important for people to control their sexuality because it causes a lot of hurt and confusion. *I hurt and need help.*"

What about the marital status of the parents? Of our teenagers, 68 percent came from homes in which their biological parents were still married and living together, 27 percent had parents who were separated or divorced, and in 5 percent of the cases one or both parents had died.

The question has often been raised as to the proportion of Adventist homes that have been broken by separation or divorce. While precise figures are very difficult to obtain, this large, representative study suggests that more than one-fourth of Adventist homes have experienced this tragedy.

To carry this line a bit further, only 65 percent of the teenagers lived with both biological parents when they were at home (discounting students at boarding schools). The other 35 percent had some other living arrangement as follows:

Live with one parent	17%
Live with one parent and one stepparent	13%
Live with adoptive parents	2%
Live with guardians	3%

For the 35 percent who no longer have both biological parents heading their homes, in about half of the cases (18 percent) the separation occurred before the child was six years old. Another 12 percent split in later childhood, with the final 5 percent happening during the teen years.

Does the structure of the family make a difference? We contrasted those from intact homes with those from divided

TABLE 2-2

Comparison of Attitudes Between TEENAGERS FROM INTACT AND DIVIDED HOMES

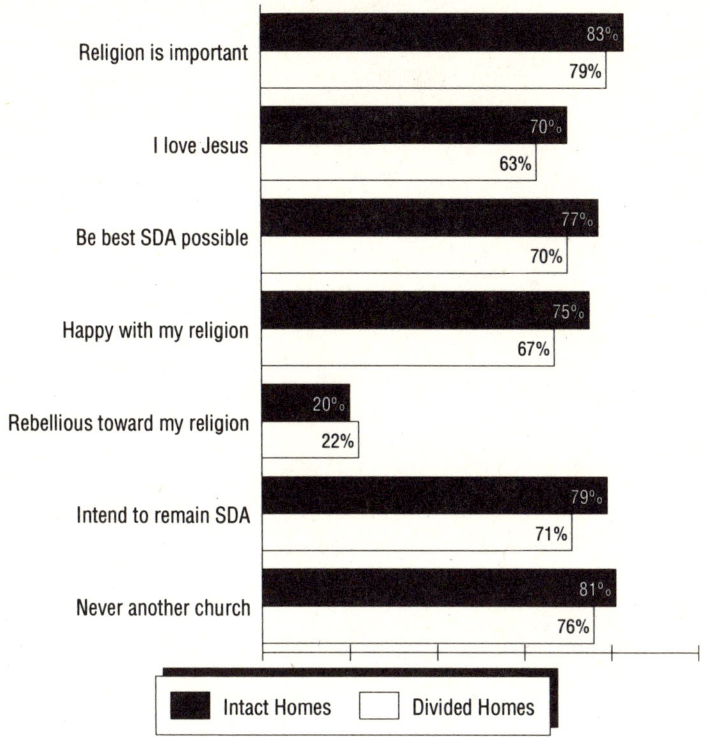

homes on the same seven key items we used for religiously divided homes. Table 2-2 shows the results.

On every item those from intact homes were more positive toward the church than those from divided homes. The spread was not great, but it ran to seven or eight percentage points on four of the items, including happiness with religion and intention to remain Adventists, a difference that is statistically significant. Those from intact homes were also significantly more likely to desire to marry Adventists.

These findings support those of Noble, who studied seniors in Adventist academies in the North Pacific Union Conference and concluded that students who come from homes divided by death, divorce, or religious difference tend to be less stable in their relationship to church beliefs and standards and more critical of the denomination's educational system.[9]

If we compare statistical nuances, having *both parents as members of the church* seems to weigh a bit heavier than having a maritally intact home. This may offer some encouragement to those Christian parents who find themselves in a divorce—perhaps not of their own choosing—and feel guilty about their parenting roles. God can still work to bring good out of a bad situation for those who love Him. Blaming oneself never helps. But the ideal remains a Christian home united in every way.

Family Influences

When we compared the relative influence of home, church, and school on the attitudes and behaviors of the teenagers, we concluded that home influences had the most impact. We asked the youth to rate certain items as to their helpfulness on the spiritual experience of the respondents. The percentages rating each item as "helpful" were as follows:

What I learned at home	85%
What I learned at church	79%
What I learned at school	54%

Another set concerned the helpfulness of the members of these families on the spiritual experience:

Home family	74%
Church family	55%
School family	35%

Finally, the spiritual commitment of the leaders of these institutions was rated for spiritual helpfulness.

Parents	70%
Pastor	66%
Teachers	50%

It should be noted that only about half of our teenagers were attending Adventist schools. Therefore, Christian-school influences did not have the opportunity to be as strong as the other two.

In any human interaction the degree of influence is at least partially determined by the closeness of the relationship. We asked the youth to rate the closeness of their relationships with eight people or groups on a five-point scale. The percentages selecting the top two ratings (very close or somewhat close) were as follows:

Mother	83%
Peers	70%
Father	68%
Sister(s)	56%
Brother(s)	55%
Adventist teachers	36%
Sabbath school teachers	35%
Church leaders	30%

Here we see that mother has a big lead when teenagers consider to whom they feel close. Father ranks third, but only about two-thirds experience that closeness with him. Perhaps it is more than coincidental that the very same percentage listed fathers who are church members. Peers rate slightly better than fathers, but other close relationships trail off significantly. We will have more to say about adult-teen relationships as a factor in holding youth for the church in a subsequent chapter.

One of the chief duties of parenthood is to aid youth in growing toward independent, responsible adulthood. When asked to what extent their parents had facilitated such growth, here is what the young people said:

	Very supportive	Usually favorable
Mothers	60%	26%
Fathers	48%	26%

Only small proportions (4-7 percent) felt that their parents tried to hold them back or were actually antagonistic.

We were interested in the perceptions of the young people as to the type of enforcement they had experienced. They rated their upbringing as follows:

	Lenient	Moderate	Strict
Overall	16%	42%	42%
Mother	25%	34%	41%
Father	19%	33%	39%

The remaining 9 percent in the last row (no doubt from mother-headed homes) said that the question of father enforcement was not applicable to them.

Finally, we wanted to know who were the spiritual role models that teenagers admired. Were there any spiritual "heroes"? The question was: "Are there any Adventists whom you admire so much that you would love to be 'just like' them, and whom you would feel terrible about if you heard that they left the church?" The proportions who answered "yes" to each class of people are as follows:

Parents	45%
Pastors	40%
Adult church members	35%
Teachers	32%
Grandparents	28%
Peers	27%
Siblings	15%

While none of the groups can claim to be spiritual heroes to a majority of the adolescents, the first-place position of parents is noteworthy. Although teenagers feel close to their peers (as pointed out above), peers do not prove to be the spiritual role models whom the teenagers actually admire—ranking not only behind parents but also behind pastors, adult church members, teachers, and grandparents.

So for weal or for woe, by a number of different measures home and parents seem to be the strongest influences on the attitudes of adolescents. We looked at religiously united versus divided homes, maritally intact versus split homes, ratings of spiritual influence, closeness of relationships, and spiritual role models. All revealed the primacy of the solid Christian home.

Finally, as stated at the beginning, when asked to complete the sentence: "The most important thing in life to me is _____, 11 percent of the teenagers said "family." This was the second-highest response—exceeded only by "God." It is interesting that many of those who chose "family" did so in the context of getting their family or some member of it to know God and be prepared for heaven.

Whether or not, then, our young people remain with Christ and His church may well depend to a large extent on what happens in the family. The paramount effort that the church can make to retain its youth is to support and nurture the Christian home.

References

[1] Ellen G. White, *The Ministry of Healing* (Mountain View, CA: Pacific Press Publishing Association, 1942), p. 349.

[2] Snell Putney and Russell Middleton, "Rebellion, Conformity, and Parental Religion Ideologies," *Sociometry* 24 (June 1961): pp. 125-135.

[3] Joan Aldous and Reuben Hill, "Social Cohesion, Lineage Type, and Intergenerational Transmission," *Social Forces* 43 (May 1965): pp. 471-482.

[4] William C. McCready, "Faith of Our Fathers: A Study of the Process of Religious Socialization" (Ph.D. dissertation, University of Illinois at Chicago Circle, 1972).

[5] Martin A. Johnson, "Family Life and Religious Commitment," *Review of Religious Research* 14 (Spring 1973): pp. 144-150.

[6] Merton P. Strommen, *Five Cries of Youth* (New York: Harper and Row, 1974), p. 85.

[7] Kevin Treston, Raymond Whiteman, and Jerry Florent, "Catholic School Training Versus Adolescent Background and Orientation: Two Comparative Studies," *Notre Dame Journal of Education* 6 (Spring 1975): pp. 59-64.

[8] Hart M. Nelsen, "Gender Differences in the Effects of Parental Discord on Preadolescent Religiousness," *Journal for the Scientific Study of Religion* 20 (December 1981): pp. 351-360.

[9] Joel N. Noble, "Certain Religious and Educational Attitudes of Senior High-school Students in Seventh-day Adventist Schools in the Pacific Northwest" (Ph.D. dissertation, University of Oregon, 1971).

CHAPTER 3

Families That Pray Together . . .

The oral defense of a doctoral dissertation was in progress. One of the examiners turned to the candidate. "You report the benefits to teenagers of family worship in your research," he said, "but personally I have found that getting teenagers interested in family worship is a *very* tough job. What do you have to say to that?"

Well said. The examiner expressed the frustration and anxiety of many parents in his question, and the fact that the concern merited interrogation at an academic defense validates the truth that the problem truly *is* regarded as *tough*. We'd like to suggest several approaches toward a solution of the problem, but first let us tell you what our study uncovered concerning family worship.

Teenagers Report

We asked these adolescents how often they participated in worship with their families. The answers were: 23 percent said "never," 27 percent said "once in a while," 8 percent said "once or twice a month," 18 percent said "once or twice a week," and 24 percent said "almost every day."

In order to show how participation in family worship or lack of it relates to other attitudes and behaviors, we have set up a series of comparisons. Since comparing five groups can be confusing, we have reduced them to two. The first includes the

58 percent who never participate or who do so only once in a while or once or twice a month. For ease in explanation we will call them the "irregulars." The second group includes the 42 percent who participate on at least a weekly basis. We will call them the "regulars."

The comparisons are enlightening. For example, the fathers of 60 percent of the irregulars but 78 percent of the regulars are baptized members of the church. The comparable figures for mothers are 87 percent and 94 percent. It is, of course, logical that worship would be more frequent in homes where a higher proportion of parents are members. The spread is greater for fathers because such a high percentage of mothers overall are members that not much room for variance remains.

How does family worship relate to church attendance? Well, 79 percent of the irregulars attend church nearly every week, but for regulars the figure is 98 percent. The fathers of 52 percent of the irregulars but 77 percent of the regulars are in church nearly every week. The comparable figures for mothers are 73 percent and 94 percent.

As to the home arrangements, only 59 percent of the irregulars, compared with 72 percent of the regulars, live with both biological parents. With regards to school attendance, 47 percent of the irregulars are currently in Adventist academies compared with 58 percent of the regulars. And 33 percent of the irregulars but 49 percent of the regulars have present plans to attend Adventist colleges. (Remember that the youth were only 15 or 16 years old at the time they completed the survey.)

We asked the teenagers to rate certain factors as to their influence on their own spiritual experience by using a five-point scale from "most helpful" to "most unhelpful." The proportions rating three family factors either "most helpful" or "somewhat helpful" were as follows: "What I learned at home"—irregulars = 72 percent, regulars = 91 percent; "The members of my home family"—irregulars = 66 percent, regulars = 86 percent; "My parents' spiritual commitment"—irregulars = 61 percent, regulars = 81 percent. The approximately 20-point spread on all three items indicates a significant difference in the spiritual impact of homes where family worship is or is not a common experience.

We also asked: "Are there any Adventists whom you admire so much that you would love to be 'just like' them, and whom you would feel terrible about if you heard that they left the church?" This question was followed by eight different classes of people. For those saying "yes" to "parents," the spread was considerable—irregulars = 38 percent and regulars = 55 percent—while the other categories revealed only small differences.

It is instructive to note how the two groups differ on attitudes toward some of the lifestyle standards of the church. In the list below the percentages refer to the proportion selecting either "somewhat agree" or "strongly agree" to each item.

	Irregulars	Regulars
Rock music	27%	39%
Dancing/discos	29%	44%
Premarital sex	59%	66%
Movie theatres	19%	33%
Recreational drugs	73%	75%
Tobacco	72%	75%
Alcohol	70%	75%
Jewelry/excessive makeup	35%	47%
Unclean meats	61%	67%

In every case the regulars are more positive toward church standards, although the differences tend to be small in temperance and health issues and large in recreational areas. Nevertheless, the consistency is remarkable.

We also asked the young people about their agreement with

a number of statements expressing attitudes toward the church and their relationship to it. While in every case the regulars were more positive than the irregulars, we have selected ten statements (given in abbreviated form) in which the difference between the two groups was 10 percentage points or more.

	Irregulars	Regulars
Intend to remain SDA in future	67%	86%
Have a love experience with Jesus	62%	75%
Want to marry an Adventist	56%	74%
Want children to attend SDA schools	54%	69%
Happy with my religion	67%	82%
Will never belong to another church	73%	87%
Adventists live what they believe	38%	50%
Want to be best SDA Christian I can	68%	85%
Have personal devotions when on own	61%	76%
SDA standards/rules are reasonable	44%	59%

Obviously, the group that is participating in family worship on a somewhat regular basis feels more at home with Adventism and is more likely to want to remain in the fellowship. In fact, 63 percent of the regulars identified themselves as "active Seventh-day Adventists" compared with 46 percent of the irregulars.

A carry-over from family worship to personal devotional practices also exists. For example, 85 percent of the regulars claimed to pray personally either almost every day or at least once or twice a week, but only 74 percent of the irregulars could make the same claim. Only 39 percent of the irregulars read their Bibles with the same frequency, but 57 percent of the regulars got into the Word on at least a weekly basis.

If we took any one of these differences by itself, it would not be strong enough to establish the superiority of regular family worship as a practice in Adventist homes. But when we put them all together, a definite "family-worship advantage" emerges. It is not safe to conclude, however, that compelling adolescents to take part in family devotions will result in their church retention. Forcing dull, lifeless family worships on teenagers might produce *un*happiness with religion. Both variables, increased family worship and stronger intentions to remain Adventists, may stem from a third variable: a stronger spiritual attitude in general or better parental role models. Or, the intentions to remain Adventists may stimulate family worship as a means to the goal.

Likewise, it is also possible that happiness with religion stimulates an increased desire for family worship. The correlations suggest relationships, not causation, and the purpose of this chapter is to aid parents in breaking into the correlation cycle at the point of family-worship.

Making Worship Relevant

How might we answer the dissertation examiner? We would suggest two basic approaches.

First, if there were any lack of interest or antagonism evident, we would lay aside the devotional book or Bible and focus on the teenager's needs. We would ask questions such as: "What was the worst thing that happened to you today?" or, in the positive vein, "What was the nicest thing that Jesus did for you today?" The first question prepares the way for parent/teenager communication, claiming the Lord's promises, and prayer; the second, for praise. An appropriate spiritual question for either situation might be, "Which Bible character do you believe felt most what you are feeling now?"

If appealing to the teenager's "felt needs" by this approach does not work and the teenager still complains that worship is *boring*, a second strategy would be to tactfully turn the priestly leadership role of conducting a worship over to the teenager. In other words, "If you don't like *our* best efforts, let's see how *you* would do it."

One set of parents was pleasantly surprised when they utilized this tactic. Their son, Ryan, was passing through the junior-high years, when adolescents acquire a physical stage that seems to transcend their maturity level. This is carried out in terms of "might makes right," or, "If you can't *make* me, don't bother telling me." Ryan's awareness of his developing muscles was intensified by his belonging to a gymnastic team that accentuated his "body beautiful" fascination even more.

Meanwhile, Ryan's fascination with his muscles was equalled by his *un*fascination with family worship. Worship was *boring* and *too long*. But when his perplexed parents turned a worship over to him to conduct, to find out what he did *not* consider boring, Ryan prepared an informative worship on *health*—how to keep the body fit and strong. In fact, he soon had Mom and Pop antidoting their lack of exercise by taking walks and had the whole family eating more healthfully, too, Mom reports. Whereas worship had heretofore been too long, according to Ryan, the family found that *his* worships were even longer!

Only that which is relevant to teenagers will arrest their interest. That which is not will be as ignored as Ezekiel's wheels or the King of the North. Teenagers may not be deliberately tuning out the devotional thoughts in family worship, but they are consumed by survival needs that adults may have long since forgotten: competitive peer pressure, the dating quest, earning grades, rules they resist, desires for a car while earning but minimum wages, et cetera. Family worship—successful family worship, that is—likely must enter *their* frame of reference and address their needs.

Most teenagers love the opportunity to talk and communicate. And those who withhold communication probably need the opportunity to be drawn out in an emotionally-safe environment. Most teenagers would also like more time with their parents. Family worship provides this time of togetherness and can foster communication leading to spiritual themes. If parents can only discover what it is that the teenager wants to talk *about*, the teenager will usually talk.

Parents, who usually feel the responsibility of raising off-spring most of their waking hours, may actually feel a relief when the teenager's concerns surface during worship. For then, especially, the role of acting as the *end authorities*, the ones with all the answers, does not rest on them, but on God. Worship is not an appropriate setting for earthly parents to intercept concerns en route the heavenly Parent by giving their own parental pronouncements on the problem. This response will close down the circuit not only to God but also to themselves as parents. Worship is a time of *leading* the teenagers to the Lord for answers, developing a pattern of experience whereby the teenagers learn to find their Source of solutions on their own. Developing this pattern of "taking it to the Lord" may be more spiritually beneficial in the long run than solving the immediate concern.

Parents who wish to utilize family worship to this end may:

1. provide an emotionally safe atmosphere in worship whereby *any* spiritual concern/problem may be introduced without revealing shock or surprise in the parents.

2. with the teenager, probe where this matter may have been dealt with in the Bible, resisting the temptation to quickly turn to a conclusive "Thus saith the Lord."

3. provide a spirit of prophecy index and suggest key words on the matter that the teenager may look up and then share the following night.

4. *pray* as a family, especially for one concern in *each* family member's life—not leaving the teenager to believe that he or she is the only one with problems and who sometimes falls short.

5. make prayer requests *specific*. The communal joy of answered prayers cannot be experienced if no one is sure exactly what the request was. "Lord, I need Your help to do better in math" is more difficult to ascertain whether an answer has been given than is "Lord, please help the tutor to be available to help

me this week so that each day my assignment can be turned in on time."

6. in the end, after exploring all the spiritual light available on the matter (Bible, spirit of prophecy, some other source, or the input of counsel from a trusted spiritual person) ask the teenager to share his/her conclusions on the matter in worship with the family.

7. once a teenager has expressed a conviction aimed in a spiritual direction, encourage, encourage, encourage, and pray, pray, pray for his/her perseverance and endurance to the desired end.

The timing of the family worship period may be critical to whether teenagers will sit on the edge of their chairs waiting for it to end. A teenager doesn't want family worship scheduled during ball practice any more than parents want it regularly scheduled during the news. A relaxing time can be agreed upon by all.

If your teenager simply resists worship "talks," try having a little musical time together (especially effective if the teenager plays an instrument) and a short prayer. Sometimes *one-liner* spiritual thoughts planted at strategic times throughout the day yield more than our best efforts at formalized worship. Teenagers are especially sensitive whether the message of worship is practiced throughout the day or if worship is just a dutiful routine by which to close the day.

A man once asked an evangelist, known to be very close to the Lord, if he could spend a day with him and observe his relationship with God. The evangelist agreed, and throughout the day the observer witnessed several periods of personal *time-out* with God. At the close of the day, the observer thought to himself, *Now comes the climax; how interesting it will be to see the finale with which this man closes his day with God*. To his surprise, the evangelist merely looked toward heaven and said, "Good-night, Lord, I'll see You in the morning."

Parents distressed with knowing where to draw the line

between firmness and force should remember a third factor—flexibility. Perhaps the best principle in regard to the use of force was given by Jesus through the prophet Jeremiah: "I have drawn you with loving-kindness" (Jer. 31:3).

Family worship during adolescence is not always a time of contention and conflict, however. As one mother said, "It was only our drawing together in family worship that pulled us through those troublesome teenage years. We talked together, prayed together, cried together, and sang together, and somehow we all got through it."

For creative suggestions to make family worship interesting for all ages, we recommend the book *Heart Tuning*, by Drs. John and Millie Youngberg, creators of the Marriage Commitment Seminar (Hagerstown, MD: Review and Herald® Publishing Association, 1985).

CHAPTER 4

Love/Hate the Church

Three young cub scouts were fishing on a riverbank when one of them fell in. The other two jumped in to save him, and after they had pulled him out, one of them ran to inform the victim's mother. "We're trying to give him artificial respiration," he sobbed, "but he keeps getting up and walking away!" At least that's how the story goes.

In spite of the church's best efforts, many youth are getting up and walking away as we feverishly try to save them. The questions are, How many? and, What is causing the problem? Are we initially using artificial *in*spiration? And when alienation does develop, are we using irrelevant methods to draw them back?

These questions plagued the North American Division researchers who designed this far-reaching study in geography and time. The next nine studies will help chart the corrective course; this first study only gave us our fixed bearings. Yet, as some sage has remarked, if we would know the direction to go, we must first know where we are. So how do these 1,511 teenagers presently relate to the church?

Religion and Membership

While all the adolescents in our sample were baptized members of an Adventist Church (a requirement for admission), only 53 percent identified themselves as *active* Seventh-day Adventists. The others were inactive or still searching before making a personal commitment. This suggests that being baptized and making a personal commitment are not necessarily synonymous.

But how do these youth *feel* about the church? After all, we human beings tend to keep doing those things that we like and avoid that which we find unpleasant. The percentages of our sample that agreed with several important attitude statements were as follows:

Religion is important in my life	82%
I have a love experience with Jesus Christ	67%
I want to be the best Adventist Christian I can possibly be	75%
I'm happy with my religion	73%
I feel rebellious toward my religion	21%

Notice that while religion in general is important to the great majority, a somewhat lesser percentage (although still high) are attached to the particular religion of Seventh-day Adventism. An even lower percentage are those who claim to be in relationship with Jesus. And, certainly, it must concern us that 21 percent felt rebellious toward their religion—especially since only 60 percent disagreed with this statement; the other 19 percent were neutral. Thus a full 40 percent are not ready to say they *don't* feel rebellious, even though many of them value religion and would like to live it.

How do these teenagers see themselves relating to the church a few years down the road? When the question was restated in terms of the future, 76 percent indicated that they intend to remain Adventists when they are on their own. This suggests that although some for now wish to practice less than they believe, three-fourths of the youth have an underlying faith in the ideal.

A number of other interesting questions were asked that required future self-projections. Table 4-1 shows the results.

TABLE 4-1
FUTURE SELF-PROJECTIONS

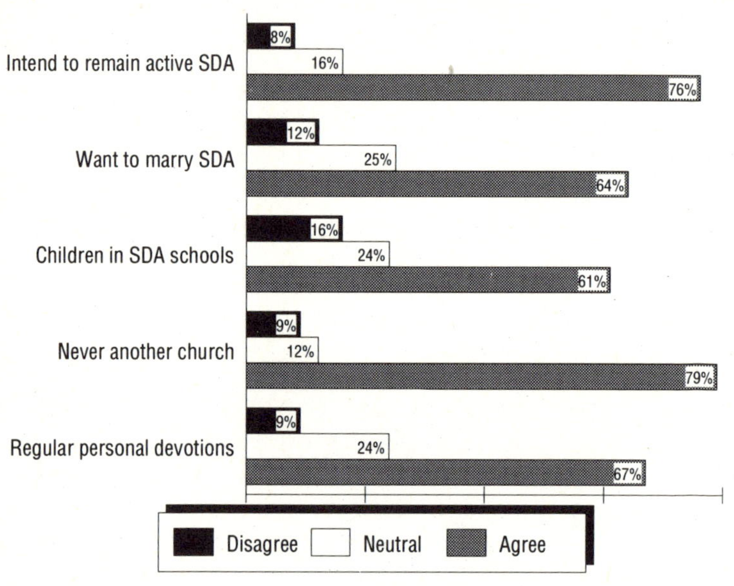

We can see here that majorities want to preserve those practices that would bind them to the church. Actual affiliation rates the highest, with personal devotions somewhat lower. A little lower yet are behaviors such as marrying within the faith and giving one's future children a Christian education—things that make it more likely one will continue a personal connection with the church. A glance at the "disagree" column, however, reveals a small core (perhaps an average of 10 percent) who are already headed for the doors, and an inspection of the middle column tips us off that a considerable proportion are sitting on the fence.

Several youth, in addition, wrote that they would like to see more expression and spontaneity in Adventist church services, such as clapping, joyfulness, and more singing. Viewed in perspective of the many youth who responded voluntarily in their free-response answers that their church is "boring," "unexciting," or "dead," this revelation suggests that teenagers may be looking for a more experiential religion.

Spiritual and Social Needs

A total of 41 percent responded positively (agreed or strongly agreed) that the church meets the spiritual needs of its youth. Another 25 percent were neutral, meaning that 66 percent reported no negativism. It cannot be assumed that "neutral" means "no deficiency," however. It may just mean that no expectations existed. And the remaining third definitely perceived that the church did *not* meet their spiritual needs.

When the regular church attenders were distinguished from the irregular attenders, it was found that to a statistically-significant degree the regular attenders expressed greater satisfaction than the irregular attenders that the church meets their spiritual needs.

It is not possible to conclude whether the church attenders are attending because their spiritual needs are met or whether their spiritual needs are met because they are attending. Nevertheless, the irregular attenders did not report the fulfillment experienced by the attenders. The same circular uncertainty exists regarding the satisfaction of social needs.

The results as to whether the social needs were perceived as being met were similar. The total positive responses were 44 percent, with the neutral category, 23 percent, bringing to 67 percent the total of those who did not report any negativism. The final third disagreed—14 percent of them strongly.

Again, the regular church attenders were distinguished from the irregular attenders and found to be more satisfied that the church fulfills their social needs than their less-present counterparts.

The impressions of church-provided activities, some spiritual and some social, are displayed in Table 4-2. Only those teenagers who actually did engage in these experiences are included in the evaluations.

Ingathering was the activity in which the greatest number had participated, followed closely by Pathfinders and collecting items for the needy. The percentages in the second and third columns cannot be directly compared with each other to determine which activities are best liked or least liked because only those who have participated gave ratings. The ratio of "likes" to "dislikes"

TABLE 4-2

ENJOYMENT LEVEL OF CHURCH ACTIVITIES

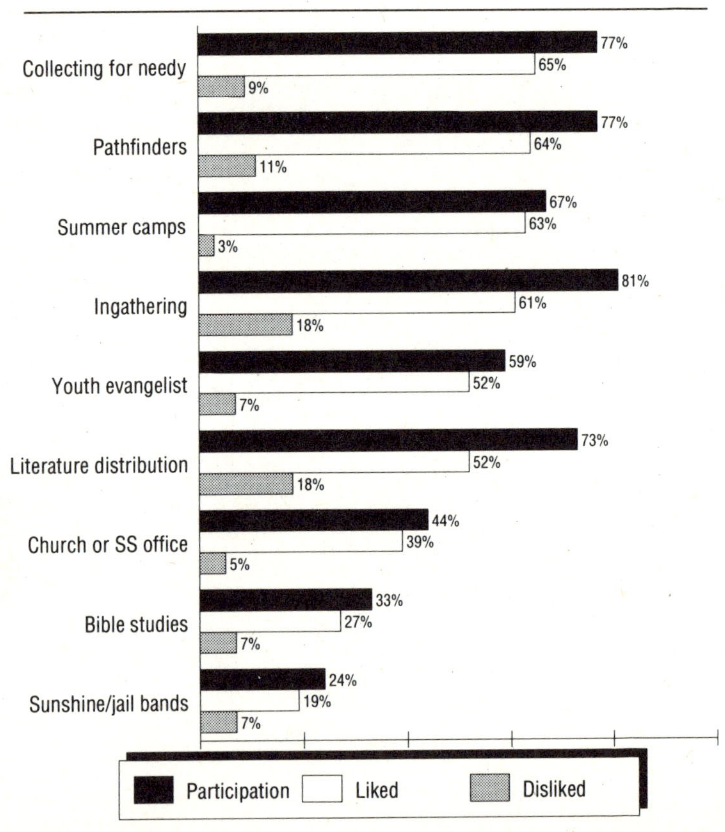

is a better comparison. Thus only 39 percent really liked serving in a church or Sabbath school office. However, since only 44 percent of the group had experienced this challenge, that 39 percent turns out to be 87 percent of those who served. This figure was higher than that for Pathfinders (85 percent), Bible studies to non-Adventists (79 percent), or Ingathering (77 percent). On this basis, most popular are summer camps (95 percent), with collecting for the needy and youth evangelistic meetings tied for second at 88 percent each. Least popular are literature distribution (74 percent) and sunshine/jail bands (73 percent).

No conclusion can be drawn as to whether the spiritual or the social factor in the Adventist Church is more important in youth attendance. We can conclude only that regular attenders report significantly greater satisfaction in both areas than irregular attenders.

Perceptions of Pastors/Members

But "church" is not just—or even primarily—an institution or a set of beliefs. Church is people, and any real measure of adolescent attitudes toward the church must take into account how these youth feel about pastors and members. We asked our teenagers: "Are there any Adventists whom you admire so much that you would love to be 'just like' them, and whom you would feel terrible about if you heard that they left the church?" The following percentages said "yes" to certain groups of people: parents, 45 percent; pastors, 40 percent; adult members, 35 percent; teachers, 32 percent; grandparents, 28 percent; peers, 27 percent; miscellaneous others, 18 percent; siblings, 15 percent.

It is significant that although teenagers reported being close to peers and siblings, those who had the strongest influence on their ideals were adults. Young people are not looking to age-mates as spiritual role models. This may cause adults to "take heart" that their influence is not as minimal compared to youth peers as they might have expected.

While none of these groups are "heroes" to the majority of our teenagers, it is encouraging that pastors are second only to parents, with other adult members in third place. While we should work to increase these percentages (more about that in another chapter), the responses show that spiritual leaders who live out their religion can make a difference.

One happy teenager expressed best the typical response that describes the type of relationships with those responsible for their spiritual welfare that teenagers prefer: "I'd like to tell you about my Sabbath school leaders. They are so incredible. I don't know anyone who can make religion so much fun. Without them I may have stopped going to church. They don't stand in front of us with Bible in one hand and chalk in the other. They sit with us in a circle and we talk. We discuss things rather than have lectures. I think it's much better for us to be asked things and talk about them, rather than to just be told, 'This is right; this is wrong; do this to go to heaven, et cetera.' "

Table 4-3 reveals the teenagers' perceptions of Seventh-day Adventist members overall. (See next page.)

We see a lot of ambivalence here. Note that 68 percent indicated positive responses to Adventists being God's chosen people and 67 percent felt that Adventists express love, whereas only 36 percent responded that Adventist lifestyles are superior and 39 percent that there is harmony among church leadership.

More than half (but not much) expressed *dis*agreement with the negative statements—that Adventists are hypocrites (51 percent), that they serve God through fear of being lost (56 percent), or that good Adventists have less fun than worldly people (57 percent). The large proportions who disagree or are neutral challenge us to find ways to communicate a vibrant, joyous Christian experience to our onlooking youth.

Perceptions of members varied. A very representative feeling expressed was, "The people have to go. Some of them come so they can find out who did this and that and what happened during the week. See who has the best, newest fashion, and which cost

TABLE 4-3

ADVENTIST TEENAGERS' PERCEPTIONS OF CHURCH MEMBERS

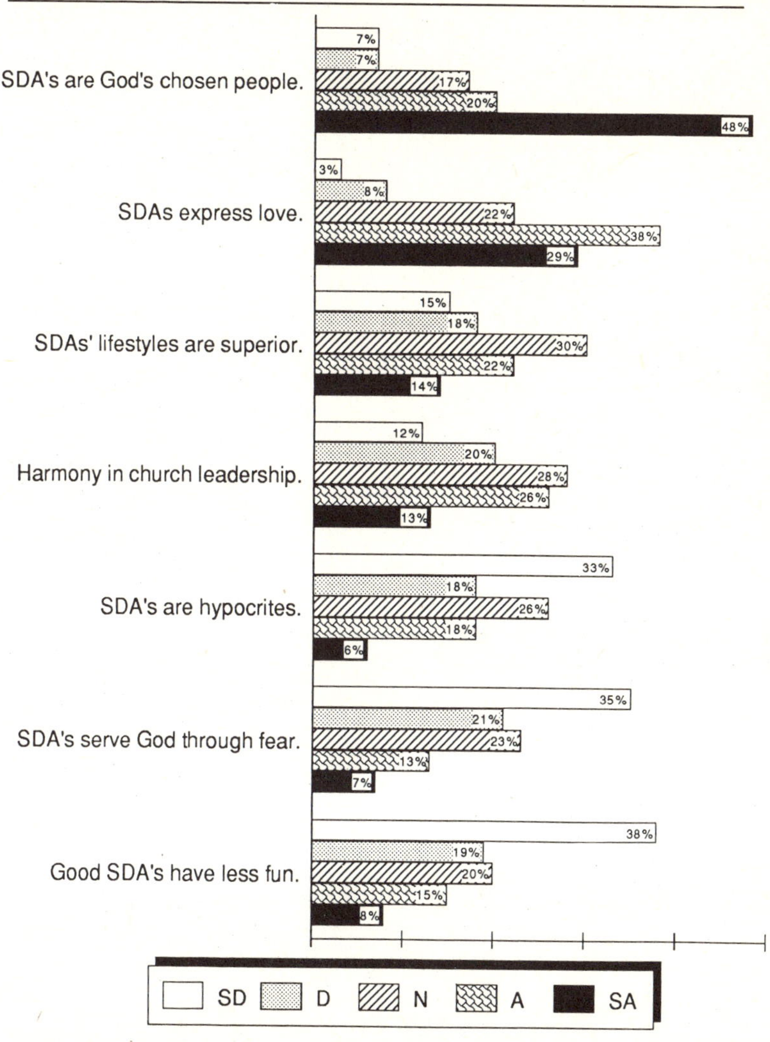

(SD = strongly disagree, D = disagree, N = neutral, A = agree, SA = strongly agree)

more, and who paid the most tithe.''

Another summarized the other end of the continuum: ''I enjoy church mostly because of the extended family it brings to me; I am so happy with our church. I hope all SDA churches are like ours. I am totally satisfied.''

It cannot be overemphasized that youth attitudes toward the church are based on perceptions of the members.

Necessity of Church Membership

Many youth expressed the sentiment that they didn't think their relationship with the church really mattered; all that matters is their personal relationship with Christ. This was usually expressed in the context of disliking the members.

One youth, who did perceive the church body essential to salvation, wrote, ''I wish we could form a new congregation at our church because I want to live with Jesus someday.''

One articulate youth wrote: ''The church has me closed into a box with many exits, but none of which pleases me.''

Another elaborated this same feeling: ''I love it, and I hate it. It holds me back. But if it didn't, things would get out of hand. So then again I like it.''

Some expressed that although they intended to remain Adventists, their Adventism would differ from the Adventism they experience today.

In summary, Adventist youth are perceiving the church through the people and are perceiving the rules through the people who make them.

If the people are warm and accepting of youth and the talents of youth, teenagers view the church as a fine place to incubate their religious experience.

If the rules are understandable, consistent, and fair, the people are viewed as spiritual role models.

If the relationships and rules represent the caring and justice of God, adolescent perceptions of the Seventh-day Adventist church are positive.

CHAPTER 5

This Is the Way We Go to Church

It seems safe to deduce that teenagers who manage to frequent football games must be there because something experienced at the stadium appeals to them. Can the same logic be applied to their church attendance—especially when the teenagers' choice to attend church may be a little less voluntary?

But sitting in a football stadium does not necessarily make one a football fan, nor does sitting in church necessarily make one a Christian—just as sitting in a hen house does not necessarily make one a chicken!

Attendance a Predictor

Yet church attendance has something going for it. We took the strength of the adolescents' intentions to remain Adventists after they were out on their own and correlated them with 27 other variables. The results were surprising. The fourth strongest predictor as to whether or not teenagers intended to remain Adventists was regular church attendance, defined in the study as *attending nearly every week*. The three variables with stronger predictive power were all personal or internal experiences: agreement with standards, frequency of personal prayer, and perceived love expressed by members. The fourth, frequency of church attendance, is a more-easily measurable experience and is probably the best objective index available to predict teenagers' intentions to remain Adventists.

It should be noted that we have been talking only about *intentions to remain Adventists*. These intentions do not imply that the youth are *happy* with their religion, nor can we assume that the Adventism they envision themselves belonging to in the future will be the same as the Adventism we are teaching them today. Perhaps we have indoctrinated them well enough so that they cannot accept another denomination's teachings, and thus they will stay with Adventism. But this does not guarantee a love relationship with Jesus Christ.

Yet church attenders are more likely to be positive in a number of ways. We divided our sample into two groups: those who say they attend church nearly every week (1,313 of them) and those who claim to attend less regularly (198). Of this latter group, 13 percent never attended, 47 percent attended "once in a while," and the remaining 40 percent attended once or twice a month. Of course, we do not know to what extent coercion is involved in the great majority (88 percent) who say they attend weekly.

At any rate, we compared the two groups on the proportions who agreed with nine key statements. Table 5-1 shows the results. Note that regular attenders are more positive on all items, with the smallest spread being 21 percentage points. The item on future intentions to remain in the church is especially dramatic with a spread of 38 percentage points.

Plausible Reasons

It must not be concluded, however, that the teenagers' dedication to Adventism will be increased by roughly 20 to 40 percent if we force them to attend church. Attendance functions here merely as an index as to whether the youth are church enjoyers or church avoiders—much as youth who appear at the football stadium are usually fans whereas those who stay away may be identified as not so interested in football or as downright non-fans.

TABLE 5-1

Comparison of Religious Attitudes Between REGULAR AND IRREGULAR CHURCH ATTENDERS

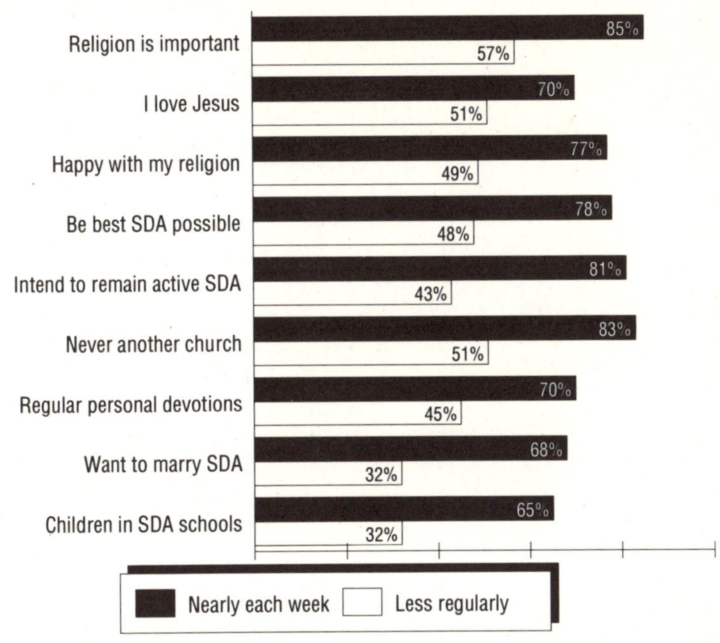

Note: All percentages are the combined percentages of those who agree strongly or agree somewhat with the statement.

Why does attendance seem to be a strong predictor? It might be that teenagers with weak intentions to remain Adventists are *already finding ways to skip*. If they come from spiritually weak homes, this avoidance may not be difficult for them.

On the other hand, some teenagers from spiritually strong homes may likewise own feelings of lack of interest or rebellion but may find it more difficult to avoid attendance with the family. Conscientious parents may read that God chose Abraham "so that he will direct his children and his household after him to keep the way of the Lord by doing what is right and just" (Gen. 18:19) and may conclude that forced exposure to the worship environment will result eventually in Christian commitment.

True, it is possible that some teenagers with no interest whatever in football may slowly acquire a taste for it if their parents consistently drag them to the stadium, and the same could possibly happen with church. But in both instances revulsion is much more likely. If we wish this demonstrated relation between attendance and positive attitudes to work for us, we will have to find ways to *attract* the adolescents to the services.

And positive role-modeling can help. The influence of the church attendance of the parents has been found in a 1978 multi-denominational study (Catholics, Southern Baptists, and Methodists) to effect a positive influence on tenth-graders.[1]

Attendance for Social Reasons

We cannot say for certain that teenagers in frequent attendance express positiveness primarily for spiritual reasons. The only safe deduction is that *some*thing, either spiritual or social, is happening at the church that brings them back regularly.

In 1972 Merton Strommen and associates reported that the "best predictor" of whether a youth will remain in the church is the degree to which the youth "belongs" or fits in.[2] As early as 1963 Strommen recognized the social element when he made observations relating the absentees with "irreligious" youth. These youth have the same basic longings and aspirations as those who are active, but the main barrier lies in their feelings of not really being wanted, their mistrust of the church, and their lack of confidence in its competence to provide help.[3]

Six years after a 1962 Billy Graham crusade in New York, a follow-up study revealed that the most important influence bearing on teenage retention was the acquisition of new friends.[4] Conversely, Warren Hartman, who conducted a Methodist study, reported in 1976 that the motivation to separate from the church was failure to feel accepted, loved, and wanted.[5] Mary Consuela reported in 1979 that Catholic youth slip away from the church for lack of identity with it—the absence of a sense of roots.[6]

In 1975 Davidson also recognized the prominence of church attendance as a measure of religiosity, when he suggested replacing the classic "Glock model"—with its complicated measuring of the ideological, ritualistic, experiential, intellectual, and consequential dimensions of religion—with a simple index: two years of regular church attendance.[7] And Hartman, in his Methodist study, reported a year later that Sunday school attendance was the best predictor of whether youth would stay in or separate from the church.[8]

And so the results of the Adventist youth study shouldn't seem surprising. These conclusions have been recognized by the Christian world for at least 25 years.

Encouraging Attendance

Suppose you were suddenly offered a million dollars if you could produce just one of your church's absentee-prone teenagers in church for at least half the Sabbaths of the year—by persuasion, of course, not by force. Wouldn't you lie awake nights wondering how to accomplish this? How long would it take to brainstorm some creative ideas? Your list probably would be even longer than the following one:

- During the week set up transportation arrangements so that pickup is automatically expected.
- Delegate an unofficial hospitality committee among the youth—insist on it.
- Invite him or her to participate in the program or to fill some special need of expertise (sound system, music, Sabbath school participant, charge of goal device). This instills a sense of belonging and value in addition to the commitment of being present to perform the duty.
- Do something unrelated to religion during the week to show a special interest in the teenager (for example, stop by and help weed his yard, teach her to sew a new dress, play a game of

ball, invite the teenager to go with you some place out of town).

- Show a continuing interest in the teenager's ambitions for the future, along with faith that the teenager can so perform.
- Call when absent to say, "I missed you" and have peers call also.
- Help the teenager discover his/her spiritual gifts. Each one has a spark of talent to develop, and some need this boost in the group because others are already well on their way to confidence in their abilities.
- Do not pressure participation in missionary activities the teenager personally dislikes, such as Ingathering. Putting unwilling members of any age on a guilt trip to do a Christian "duty" is always counterproductive in the long run.
- If the teenager is from a spiritually weak home (for instance, TV likely to be on during Sabbath hours), arrange for him/her to spend the remainder of Sabbath in a spiritually stable home.
- Develop a one-to-one relationship so the teenager can open up his/her heart.
- Pray for the teenager's attendance every Friday night so that on the Sabbath morning that the teenager does appear you can warmly say, "I prayed just last evening that *you* would be here today, and here *you* are!"

If you do all these things, you won't really win a million dollars. But you may get something even more satisfying—the satisfaction of seeing an adolescent make a long-term commitment to Christ and His church. And you may make a young friend for eternity.

References

[1] Dean R. Hoge and Gregory H. Petrrillo, "Development of Religious Thinking in Adolescence: A Test of Goldman's Theories," *Journal for the Scientific Study of Religion* 17 (June 1978): pp. 139-154.

[2] Merton P. Strommen, Milo L. Brekken, Ralph C. Underwager, and Arthur L. Johnson, *A Study of Generations* (Minneapolis: Augsburg Press, 1972), p. 295.

[3] Merton P. Strommen, *Profiles of Church Youth* (St. Louis: Concordia Publishing House, 1963), p. 241.

[4] Frederic L. Whitam, ''Peers, Parents, and Christ: Interpersonal Influence in Retention of Teen-age Decisions Made at a Billy Graham Crusade,'' *Proceedings of the Southwestern Sociological Association* 19 (1968): pp. 154-158.

[5] Warren J. Hartman, *Membership Trends: A Study of Decline and Growth in the United Methodist Church 1949-1975* (Nashville: Discipleship Resources, 1976).

[6] Mary Consuela, ''Religious Education Forum: The Past of the Church: An Essential for the Adolescent,'' *Momentum* 10 (February 1979): pp. 13-16.

[7] James D. Davidson, ''Glock's Model of Religious Commitment: Assessing Some Different Approaches and Results,'' *Review of Religious Research* 16 (Winter 1975): pp. 83-91.

[8] Hartman, *op cit*.

CHAPTER 6

Skewered on Standards

"I believe in God, but some things get blown away—like earrings, make-up, rock, movies, sex before you're married, dances. You haven't really lived. My religion sometimes makes me feel trapped from all the above."

Just another rebellious teenager? Maybe. But there's an odd twist. This young woman added: "Though I won't follow all the rules, I just love sitting in the church."

And lest you conclude that all adolescents are up on experience and down on the standards, one male wrote: "The lifestyles and standards of the church should be lifted up."

Our mail has run the gamut from reaffirmation to revolt as more than 1,500 middle adolescents have commented on the standards and rules of the Adventist church. We found that the highest correlation with intentions to remain Adventists when they are on their own was with the *degree of concurrence with Adventist standards*.

Teenagers Face Off With the Standards

We offered a five-point scale and asked our teenagers to respond to the statement, "Adventist standards/rules are quite reasonable." Here are the results: strongly disagree = 5 percent, somewhat disagree = 17 percent, neutral = 27 percent, somewhat agree = 29 percent, strongly agree = 22 percent. So we have roughly half in agreement, a fourth in disagreement, and the other fourth ambiguous—not a major rebellion to be sure, but not a sign that all is well either.

But the statement is couched in general terms. Next we asked them to respond on the same scale to nine specific areas. We have arranged these answers in Table 6-1 according to descending order of agreement. In every case but that of jewelry/makeup the wording of the table is identical to that of the questionnaire. In the one exception the questionnaire read "decorative jewelry or excessive makeup." For ease of comparison we have combined the two disagree and the two agree categories.

TABLE 6-1

Attitudes Toward
SPECIFIC ADVENTIST STANDARDS

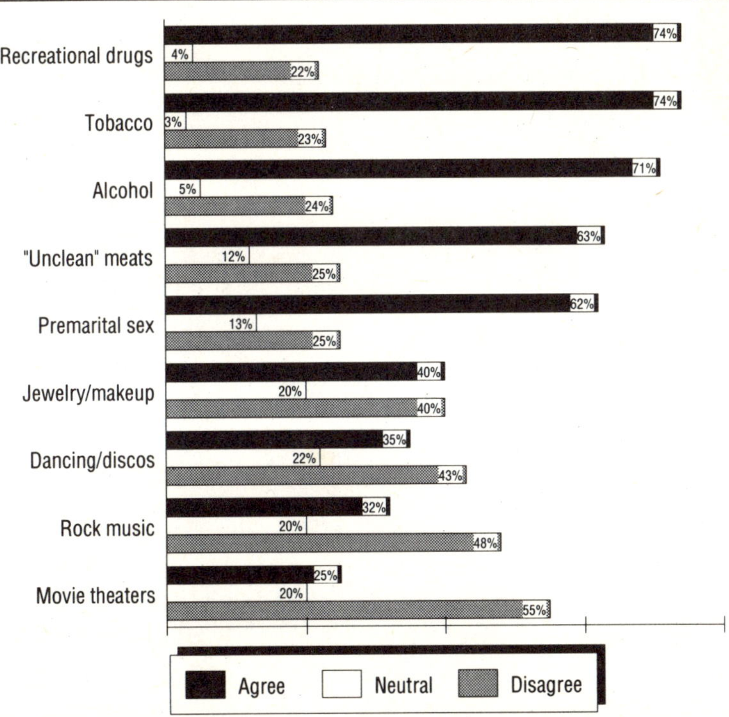

The health and temperance workers among us will be pleased to note that the most agreement comes on these issues. The majority of Adventist youth still recognize the reasonableness of our position on avoidance of various chemical substances. Whether their behavior will match their beliefs cannot be determined from the present data. Still, the church must be concerned to discover that about a fourth of its teenagers either disagree or are uncertain about its traditional health teachings, even though these have been so strongly confirmed by modern science.

We also find it alarming that only 62 percent agreed with the Adventist position on premarital sex. In fact, the figures are almost identical with that for vegetarianism. This would seem to reflect the inroads of societal changes, often called the sexual revolution. While we have no comparable data for a generation ago, we suspect that these figures represent a radical erosion in what is morally acceptable.

Five years earlier, Dudley and Dudley surveyed 247 teenagers along with their parents in an Intergenerational Value Survey.[1] In the earlier study 62 percent also agreed with the Adventist position on premarital sex, but at that time 19 percent were neutral and 19 percent disagreed. The present study represents a shift of 6 percent from neutral to disagree.

This shift is especially noteworthy because the earlier study qualified the statement by saying that "premarital sexual intercourse is not wrong *if two people really love each other*." The present study did not contain the qualifier, yet still revealed a shift in the permissive direction.

In spite of major defections, however, a majority continued to agree with the first five items. On the last four items, to the contrary, a majority were not in agreement, two-fifths or more disagreed, and there were significant neutral blocks. Movies, rock music, dancing, and jewelry—in that order—seem to be the "big four" areas where consensus with the stated church position is lacking.

Some will no doubt say that these are not character issues and should not be a part of our church standards in the first place. While it is not our purpose to either defend or attack our traditional guidelines in these areas, they are well-known and longstanding as part of what it means to be an Adventist. Therefore, opposition to them may be symbolic of a psychological separation from the church—the hinge upon which swings the future status of the young person as to church retention or dropout. This will become more apparent as we examine some correlations later in this chapter.

Of particular interest is the attitude toward movie theaters. Here only a fourth agreed with the Adventist position, and, for the first time, a majority disagreed. In the 1983 survey this was also true, but, in addition, only about 44 percent of the parents agreed, with about 46 percent in disagreement.[2] In the face of cable TV, videos, and campus-approved films, the traditional Adventist stand on movies appears to be a lost cause.

Are those who attend Adventist academies more likely to be favorable to the standards than those in public high schools? We compared the responses of the 773 academy students with those of the 634 public high attenders. To the statement, "Adventist standards/rules are quite reasonable," 52 percent of the academy students agreed as compared to 49 percent of those in high school. Very little difference between the two groups arose in response to this general statement. But what about the specific standards? The comparison is shown in Table 6-2.

There *are* differences, and in every case the academy students expressed more agreement. Differences on the health and temperance issues averaged around 10 percentage points, as did differences regarding dancing/discos. Largest of all was the difference on premarital sex. Even movie theaters showed a moderate difference. But the groups were quite close on jewelry/makeup, and virtually the same on rock music. These data may provide challenges and directions for Adventist educators.

We also asked the teenagers to respond to the open-ended

TABLE 6-2

Comparison of Attitudes toward STANDARDS BETWEEN ACADEMY AND PUBLIC HIGH STUDENTS

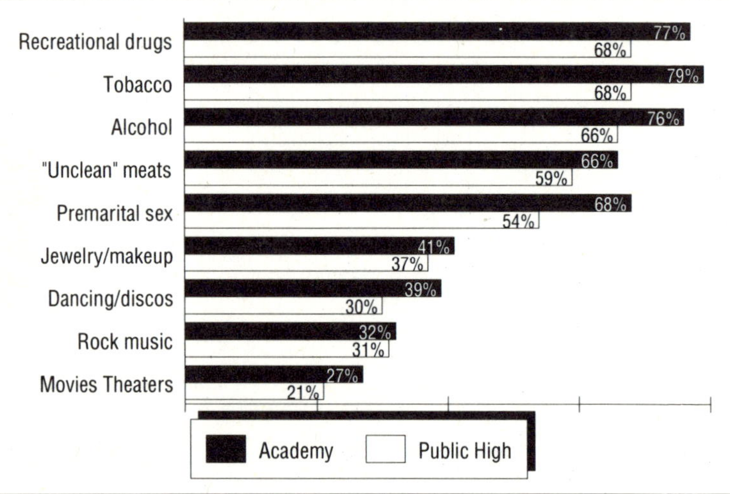

773 teenagers attending Adventist academies (451-day and 322-boarding)
634 teenagers attending public high school

statement: "The first thing I would like to change about my religion is ______." Although the most popular response (27 percent) was "nothing," 12 percent indicated "relax strictness," and another 10 percent indicated "standards." In coding these categories, we used "standards" to designate the principle involved and "strictness" to denote the degree to which the standards are enforced. On the other hand, 8 percent called for "more commitment."

One young man wrote: "My religion has high standards, and I'm for high standards."

Standards and Retention

Given the chief purpose of this 10-year study, perhaps the most important question was "I intend to remain an active

Adventist when I am on my own.'' To this item 76 percent agreed (56 percent of them strongly), 16 percent were uncertain, and only 8 percent disagreed. Of course, it may not turn out that way 10 years from now, but it is the first indication of the thinking of these youth. It will be interesting to compare the actual destiny of these young people with their present aspirations. In the meantime we can compare their intentions with other variables to see what might best predict their adult status vis-a-vis the church.

Using various statistical techniques, we correlated several dozen variables with the future-intentions statement. The highest correlation (.52) was with the item on agreement with Adventist standards. Those teenagers who agree that Adventist standards and rules are quite reasonable are more likely to affirm their intentions to remain Adventists when they are on their own than those who disagree with the standards and find them unreasonable.

Of course, a strong relationship between these two variables does not determine the direction of influence or even prove that one causes the other. But logic would suggest that those who find the standards to their liking would naturally decide to ''stay with the ship,'' whereas those who are unsatisfied might well be thinking of ''going overboard.'' This likelihood challenges the church to discover fresh methods of presenting its standards to the next generation so that these standards will be perceived as reasonable and beneficial. If we find no way to do that, perhaps we need to reexamine them to see if they really reflect what is essential in Adventist theology.

Influences on Attitudes Toward Standards

Two other significant correlations with standards are worth noting, although they are not nearly as strong as the one just mentioned. Those adolescents who perceive that they have experienced stricter enforcement in the growing-up process from parents and teachers are slightly more likely to agree with the standards than those reporting lenient enforcement. This surprised us. We expected to find the opposite, given the adolescent struggles for emancipation and the consequent tendency to rebel. Perhaps the modeling influence of strict but sincere homes somewhat offsets the rejection tendency.

We should also mention that the variable "agreement with standards" was constructed by adding attitudes toward various specific standards. An examination of its components revealed that the strength (though slight) of the correlation came from alcohol and drugs, vegetarianism, and premarital sex. The three components of dancing/discos, rock music, and movies were *not* correlated with the overall perceived degree of enforcement. And, in a related finding, adolescents who perceived *restraint* in the emancipation process were more likely to feel rebellious against their religion.

On the second correlation, those teenagers who perceive that adult Adventists live up to what they believe are slightly more likely to agree with church standards than those who see the adults as largely hypocritical. This supports much previous research showing that the example of religious authority figures impacts positively or negatively on youth religiosity.[3]

Another point, which will be discussed more fully in chapter 11 but which has some relevance here, concerns the effects of reading material written by Ellen White. Of those teenagers who read her regularly, 70 percent felt that Adventist standards/rules are quite reasonable, whereas only 45 percent of those who rarely or never read her felt that way. Given the crucial relationship between retention and attitudes toward standards, a difference of 25 percentage points is worthy of further exploration.

Previously, we compared attitudes toward church standards between those attending Adventist and public schools. This had to do with *present location*. We also correlated years of attendance at Adventist schools with agreement with church standards to see if *time spent* at these institutions made a difference. We did find that those who attended longer were more likely to affirm the standards, but the relationship was slight. Present attendance seems to be more influential than total number of years in Adventist schools.

Some Suggestions for Presenting Standards

Since how teenagers feel about church standards is so intertwined with their future intentions for remaining in or leaving the church, this area should challenge our best thinking. Also teenagers are interested in standards and ready to discuss them at the drop of a hat (much more so than to discuss abstract doctrines). We have the readiness factor going for us.

Therefore, at this point we would like to offer a few suggestions that arise out of our personal experiences. We offer these with considerable humility, for we know how difficult and sticky this task is. And we recognize that it is much easier to write about this subject from behind the safety of our computers than it is to actually face and convince the youth on the "front lines." Still, with these *caveats* in mind, we would like to venture forth and, hopefully, to stimulate some thinking.

Adults can began by actualizing the instruction methods that teenagers prefer. It is a long-established fact that adolescents do not enjoy sermons and lectures—with the possible exception of those presented by a rare youth pastor with more-than-usual interest-holding qualities (charisma, humor, et cetera).

Bible teachers need not feel pressured to spend long class periods providing religious entertainment, because teenagers are really asking for discussion and involvement. Family worship might be a discussion of spiritual applications to the problems of the day, not just the reading of a passage from a religious book.

A disarming approach might be to assure the young people that God *does* believe in jewelry, dancing, and movies. God-approved jewelry was worn by the high priests (gold wires worked into the linen, onyx stones on the ephod, twelve precious stones on the breastplate with pure gold chains, gold bells between the pomegranates around the robe's hem, and a holy crown of pure gold). Many crowns will be worn by Christ when He comes; He will place star-studded crowns on the redeemed; and heaven's gates, mansions, and streets will glow with jewels. These instances might be compared with the examples of offensive jewelry in the Bible to discover the principles behind the difference, with the discussion culminating in the biblical acceptance of jewelry that denotes a state of supreme holiness —the only state worthy of drawing attention.

A discussion of dancing might begin by acknowledging the God-approved dancing performed by David, comparing his state of holy joy with the dancing that meets with biblical disapproval —the Israelites around the golden calf and the priests of Baal on Mount Carmel with their drunkenness and orgies. The teenagers could discuss whether today's dancing with today's music is expressing holy joy to the Lord or self-indulgence and lust.

As for movies, God himself will show a movie to the universe at the third coming of Jesus, a panoramic replay in the sky of the fall of Lucifer in heaven, the disobedience in Eden, and the outworking of sin in history that led to the death of Christ on the cross, the glorious Second Coming, and the present moment of the destruction of the wicked. He also showed Moses, Paul, and Ellen White pre-runs of heaven, and Moses and Elijah a cinema of the crucifixion as they visited Jesus at the transfiguration. Again, the issue is decided by the *quality* of the experience involved. Discussion questions might be whether one can avoid "bad" movies like bad novels while at the same time not rejecting all films and all books; how different types of films affect one physically, mentally, emotionally, and spiritually; and the criteria a Christian would use in selecting entertainment.

In discussing standards with teenagers, it is important not simply to fall back on codes of behavior as if they were sacred and unchangeable. Instead, we should help young people search for principles by which they can make their own mature decisions.

The standards we have addressed here afford the opportunity

to get into deep spiritual truths such as holiness (justification and sanctification), the state of holy joy, and character building through inner purity. The discussions may also lead into the effect our behavior has on others—one of the highest levels of morality.

We should realize, however, that such an approach has its dangers. We might discover that we have been inconsistent in our application of principles. We might find that we can formulate no good reason for some of our rules. The youth may back us into a corner from which we cannot extricate ourselves without appealing to tradition. We may be compelled to join the youth in rethinking why we do what we do. It is not as comfortable to be a searcher as to be an authority.

And, as a church, we will need to be aware of own failure to do what we ask of the young people. Although adults criticize the music, movies, and dress of teenagers, they often make exceptions for themselves. These inconsistencies are apparent to adolescents, who in turn can rationalize their own behavior, citing adult hypocrisy. Many of the young people in our study reflected confusion rather than conflict as they reacted to the standards. Why is a certain practice condemned while another that seems quite similar is OK? We dare not expect more from our youth than we are willing to give.

Adults and teenagers might discuss together the need for standards. One approach might be to pretend that no standards presently exist and ask the youth to begin from zero with a list they would formulate for their own future offspring. Such discussions must be handled skillfully—asking (in a nonthreatening and unhurried atmosphere that is characterized by mutual good will) the young people for both the positive and negative sides for each standard discussed. The pluses and minuses could be listed on a chalkboard as the teenagers themselves mention them. Adults should not attempt to manipulate the discussion toward predetermined ends—a technique of which adolescents are extremely wary.

Perhaps most importantly adults can develop a one-to-one relationship with a teenager—remembering that given the chance, a teenager likes to talk, discuss, confide, and communicate with a person who is really caring and interested. Taking one teenager out alone for french fries and a soft drink, allowing the opportunity for opening up the heart without peers around, is probably more productive than taking a carload to the baseball stadium.

Yes, even this approach is risky. But if the attitudes of the teenagers toward the standards of the church really determine how likely they are to remain in its fellowship as they reach adulthood, then it is even more risky *not* to make ourselves vulnerable and open a continuing dialogue. We cannot continue with "business as usual," standing by the ancient and immovable codes, if we wish to have a future for our church. Even if the historical standards turn out to be best after all, they will have to be re-created by this generation.

References

[1] Roger and Peggy Dudley, "Adventist Values: Flying High?" *Ministry*, April 1985, pp. 4-7.

[2] *Ibid.*, p. 7.

[3] See Roger L. Dudley, *Why Teenagers Reject Religion and What to Do About It* (Washington, DC: Review and Herald Publishing Association, 1978), chapter 6.

CHAPTER 7

Young Disciples

In His Great Commission Jesus combined baptism, discipleship, and witness: "All authority in heaven and on earth has been given to me. Therefore go and make disciples of all nations, baptizing them in the name of the Father and of the Son and of the Holy Spirit, and teaching them to obey everything I have commanded you. And surely I am with you always, to the very end of the age" (Matt. 28:18-20).

Baptism, discipleship, and witness are still interconnected—for teenagers as well as older folk. And now as then, each is made possible by His abiding presence. In this chapter we would like to discuss the meaning of baptism for our teenagers, the process of their discipleship, and something about the effects of their witness.

Remembering Their Baptism

Being a baptized member of the Seventh-day Adventist Church was one of the criteria for selection in our sample. So all these adolescents had participated in this experience. However, all did not perceive baptism in the same way when they were baptized, nor did all, as they looked back on the event, interpret it the same.

The prime years for being baptized were ages 10 to 12. More than half (55 percent) entered the water during this period.

Roughly 18 percent were younger than 10, and the remaining 27 percent were baptized during their early teens.

When asked for the main reason for their being baptized, 59 percent said they had made a personal choice and had requested it. This seems quite encouraging, given the stories about adult and peer pressure. But 18 percent said they just automatically accepted their parents' religion, and another 9 percent went along because the pastor had formed a baptismal class, and it was expected that the whole group would be baptized. The remaining 14 percent had a variety of other reasons.

Although the first bit of news is hopeful, that about 40 percent of our youth are being baptized without a careful, considered choice on their part is challenging, if not disconcerting.

We then asked the teenagers if they wished they hadn't been baptized, and if so why they felt that way. Many were positive about the event—59 percent said the question did not apply to them; they were glad they had done it. It is interesting to note that when the question was restated in terms of the future, 77 percent indicated that they intended to remain Adventists when they were on their own. This suggests that although some wish for now to practice less than they believe, there seems to be an underlying faith in the ideal by at least three-fourths of our youth.

Of the 41 percent who wished they hadn't been baptized, a number of interesting reasons were offered. "I was too young to understand the significance," lamented 19 percent. Others admitted, "I find myself bucking the system sometimes, or wishing I could" (10 percent) and "I question some Adventist teachings or practices" (7 percent). Those in these categories have indicated that they cannot handle their post-baptism need for continued guidance by themselves.

Some youth indicated a need for rebaptism even though they were but a few years beyond their original commitment. Typical statements were, "I want to get rebaptized, but I need further Bible studies first"; "I want to get rebaptized, I feel so sinful";

"I was too young to know what baptism means"; and "I want to get rebaptized, but I must first find my way back to the Lord and I don't know how."

These statements reveal a lack of understanding the developmental nature of sanctification and the purpose of the Lord's Supper. It thus appears that the youth may have been prepared more for baptism itself than for life *after* baptism. When the realization settles in that they have lost their "once holy" state, they conclude that they have "blown it" and must start all over.

Now that these young people are members of Christ's body, how do they rate their Christian walk? Our question produced the following results: "I am an active Seventh-day Adventist"—53 percent; "I am an inactive Seventh-day Adventist"—19 percent; "I don't have a religious philosophy, and it doesn't worry me"—3 percent; "I don't have a religious philosophy yet, but I am searching"—17 percent; "I intend to compare Adventism with other denominations before I fully commit myself (even though I am baptized)"—8 percent.

Although the questionnaire called for no response as to what other religions the latter might find worthy of investigating, a few volunteered the direction they would like to explore. It seems significant that the half dozen or so who wrote down their intentions *all* named *Pentecostalism*. No other type of Christianity or denomination was suggested. While the number is too small to serve as a basis for any major conclusions, it tends to support other evidence already cited that some youth are seeking a religion with heavier emotional overtones.

So slightly over half of these baptized adolescents are active in the church, happy with their faith, and planning to stay with it. But nearly a fourth already express open rebellion or inactive membership. And between these two groups lies our challenge—another fourth who, although baptized, appear to be either unsettled about some aspect of their religion or, at best, are still in the process of stabilizing their commitments.

The Learning Disciple

Disciples must learn "everything" that Jesus taught. Under what conditions is this learning most effective? Is the nature of the message or the personality of the messenger more powerful in the conveyance of truth? Although we asked the youth for the more important reason, some checked both. But we were surprised that 72 percent said that learning the plan of salvation was why they enjoyed religious instruction, and only 17 percent picked admiration for teacher or preacher as the single reason. We know from other evidence that youth do experience religion in relationships, and the above finding does not annul this. It rather speaks to the basic good sense and high idealism in the majority of our adolescents. By the way, 11 percent said that they *never* enjoy religious instruction.

But what about specific methods? We presented the youth with six avenues for learning doctrines and asked them to rate them on a five-point scale from "excellent" to "can't stand." The results are shown in Table 7-1.

If we combine the "excellent" and "pretty good" categories to yield an "I-like-it" rating, "talking to someone I like" leads the list with nearly three-fourths approval, followed by Sabbath school classes with 59 percent. Taking these two leading responses, we may infer that the teenager prefers verbal interaction—another indication that teens experience religion in relationships. That the least-preferred method (correspondence courses) involves no individual interaction—at least not on a face-to-face, oral basis—confirms this conclusion. The further removed the opportunity is for the youth to ask questions and participate in discussion, the less likely they are to accept the teaching method.

The Witnessing Disciple

The disciple not only learns the teachings of Jesus and accepts the baptism of water, but he or she also follows the Master in

TABLE 7-1

PREFERENCES FOR LEARNING DOCTRINES

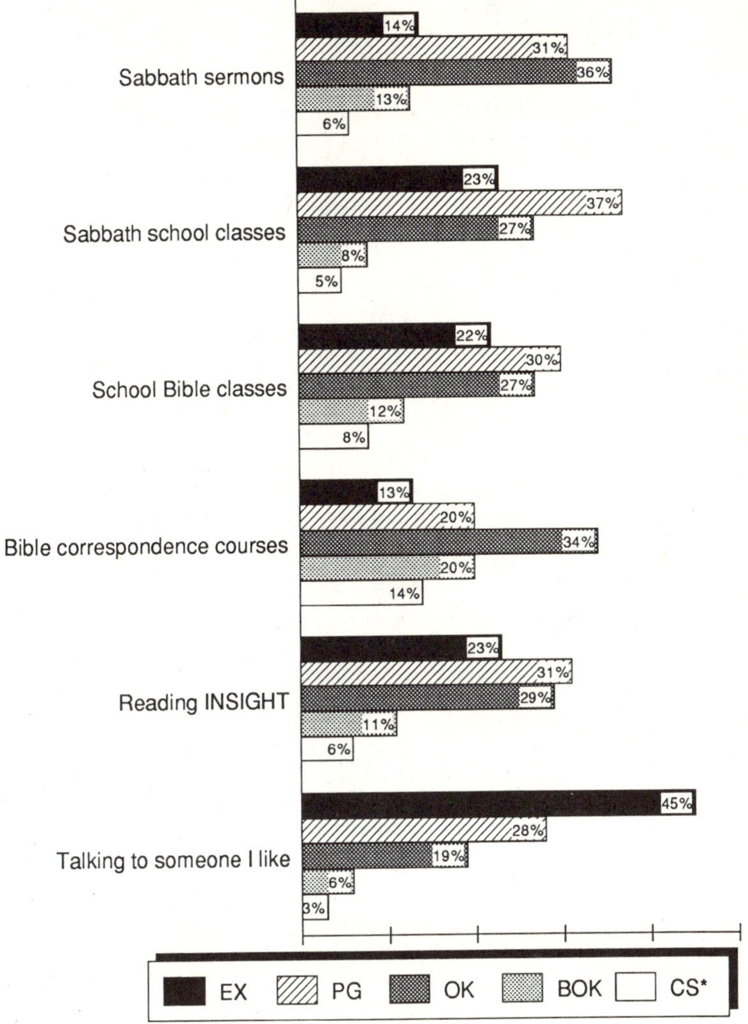

service. Discipleship calls for a commitment to Christ, to the body of believers, and to the needy world.

The youth were asked how often they had participated in nine church events. They were also asked which ones they mostly enjoyed and which ones they mostly disliked, but these findings were discussed in another chapter. Here we are interested in what they did and how often they did it. The list is displayed in Table 7-2.

The majority had never participated in three of the nine items. That two-thirds had never given Bible studies to non-Adventists is not surprising. The response from adult Adventists would probably not be much better. And given their tender years, that over half had never held a church or Sabbath school office could be expected. It is more eye-opening to find that three-fourths have never gone on a sunshine band. Those of us brought up in a previous generation thought *everybody* did that! Apparently, there is still room to make an old program into a new adventure.

When it comes to multiple experiences, Ingathering is a clear winner in terms of participation. Nearly half have been out knocking on doors or caroling five times or more, and another 15 percent have gone Ingathering three or four times. Only 61 percent, however, said they mostly enjoyed the experience, and participation in Ingathering was not significantly correlated with the extent to which the respondents affirmed that the church meets the social needs of its young people. Perhaps some of them, like one of the authors, were *made* to go.

Literature distribution, collecting items for the needy, and Pathfinders come next as activities where half of the youth have participated at least three times (three years for Pathfinders).

We might try to divide these activities into those which are mainly witness and outreach and those which are mainly within the body of believers. Looked at this way, youth evangelistic meetings, sunshine/jail bands, Bible studies, collecting for the needy, literature distribution, and Ingathering might be classified as the former, with the other three (summer camp, church office,

TABLE 7-2

PARTICIPATION IN CHURCH ACTIVITIES

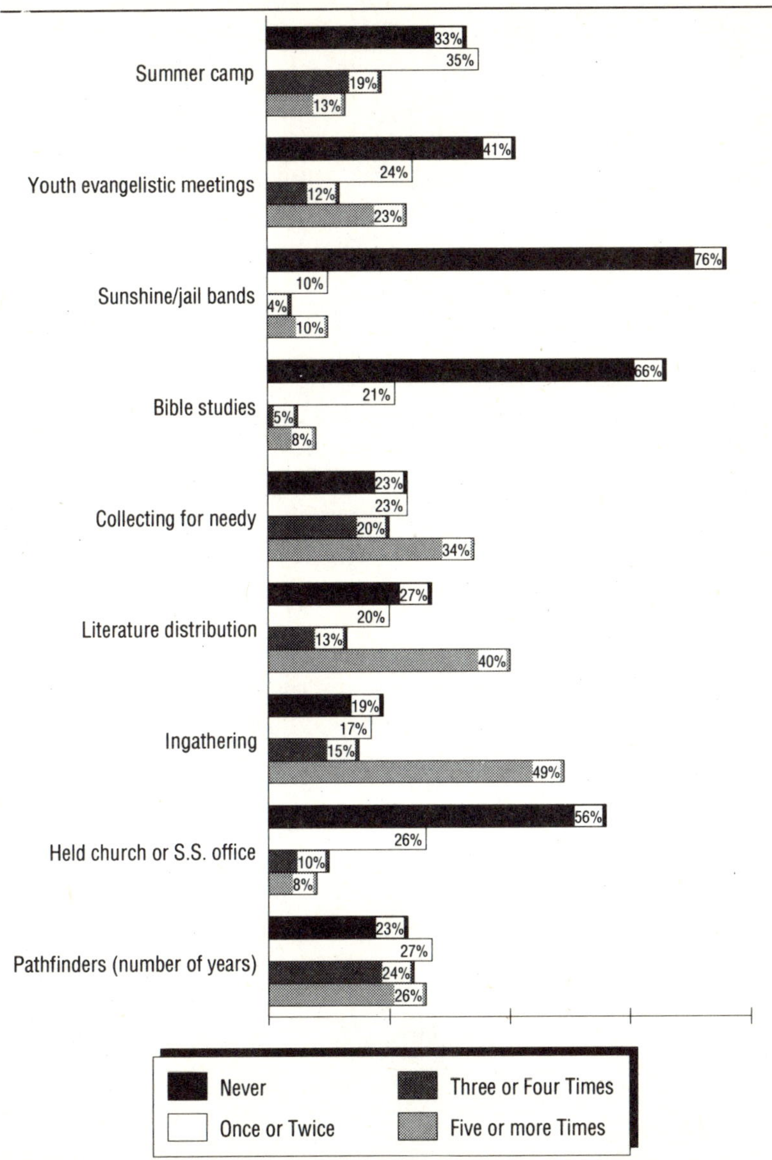

Pathfinders) in the latter class. Our adolescents seem to have kept a fair balance between outreach and nurture events.

Another question that dealt with outreach was how often the teenagers tell someone about Adventism. As shown on the table in chapter 11, the youth answered: never, 18 percent; once in a while, 49 percent; once or twice a month, 15 percent; once or twice a week, 12 percent; almost every day, 6 percent. What vibrant Christians this last group must be! Wouldn't a few of them vitalize a local congregation?

To determine how such witness is related to other attitudes toward the church, we divided the sample into two groups—those who tell others about Adventism only once in a while or never and those who do so at least monthly. We then compared the two groups on 12 key attitudes toward the church, both present and future. The comparisons can be seen in Table 7-3. The percentages are the combined percents of those who agree strongly or agree somewhat with the statement.

Notice that in every case the witnessers are more positive toward religion and the church than are the nonwitnessers. In four cases the differences are only 3 or 4 points, and in another the spread is only 7 points. But in the remaining seven items, at least 11 and as many as 15 points separate the two groups. These differences are on crucial items such as the importance of religion, having a love experience with Jesus, happiness with one's religion, finding Adventist standards reasonable, and intending to remain an Adventist in the future.

Of course, we cannot claim that witnessing produces more favorable religious attitudes. Again, the latter may stimulate the former. But the two *are* related. This certainly suggests that it would be well to foster outreach activities among the teens. Like the proverbial man who rescued another in a blizzard and through the activity kept himself going, our teens may find that by involving themselves in active discipleship, the souls that they "save" are their own.

Spader observed that about 80 percent of the youth groups he

TABLE 7-3

Relationship of
RELIGIOUS ATTITUDES AND TELLING OTHERS ABOUT ADVENTISM

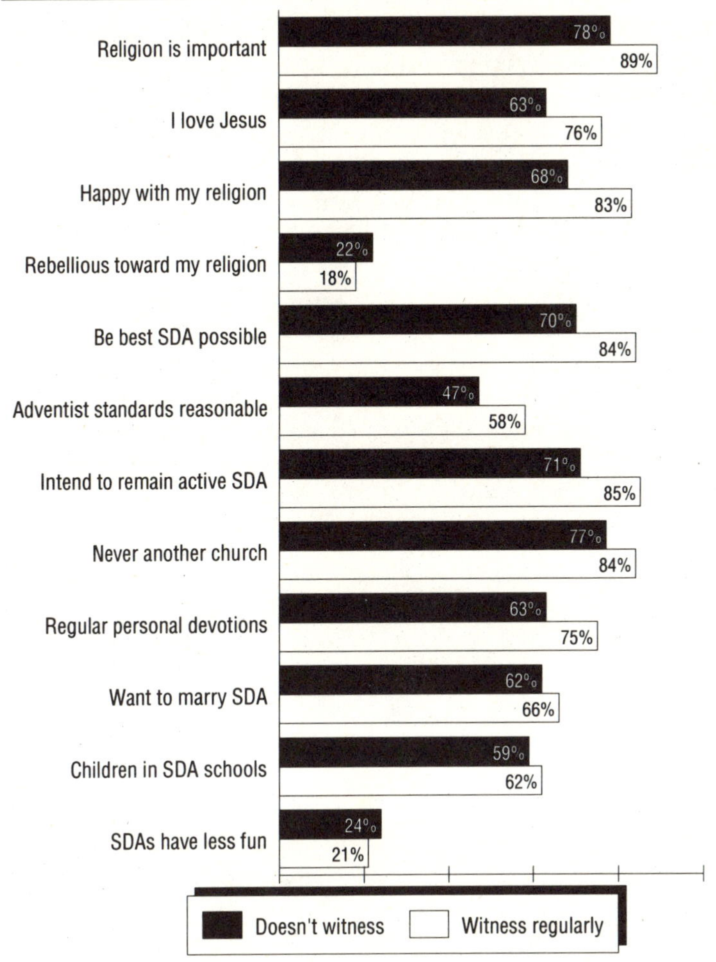

worked with had many activities at growth level—Sunday school, Bible studies, retreats, socials, quiz teams, choirs—but nothing to reach new youth through vigorous evangelism or to train committed students. Too many activities at this level can make the group become "stagnant, ingrown, cliquish," he said. Spader claimed that the young peoples' potential has been lost sight of, and adults do not really believe the youth are capable of turning around their churches and schools for the Lord.

"Teens will respond to a challenge," he concluded, "but not to some petty invitation to come and be entertained."[1]

Ellen White confirmed that the youth can be capable religious workers: "There is no line of work in which it is possible for the youth to receive greater benefit. . . .

"With such an army of workers as our youth, rightly trained, might furnish, how soon the message of a crucified, risen, and soon-coming Savior might be carried to the whole world."[2]

In planning religious activities for teenagers, one must consider them individually as well as collectively. Naden pointed out that the Holy Spirit equips each person (including adolescents) with a special gift for ministry. Discovering their spiritual gift(s) may become an exciting process for young people as they learn their potential abilities and recognize that they can perform some particular ministries better than many other people.

This could, in many cases, solve the identity crisis that teenagers experience as they are guided to find their identities in service for the Lord. In the words of Naden: "God appoints each of us to a specific ministry, something we can do happily and successfully for Him."[3]

As teenagers discover that they can be happy and successful in working for God, they will also find relief from the guilt that accompanies a perceived obligation to participate in activities they do not enjoy. As individuals minister where they feel competent, the result will be happy, contented Christians.

References

[1] Dann Spader, "Tired of Band-Aid Approaches to Youth Work?" *Moody Monthly*, January 1984, p. 56.

[2] Ellen G. White, *Education* (Mountain View, CA: Pacific Press Publishing Association, 1903), p. 271.

[3] Roy C. Naden, "Introducing the Subject of Spiritual Gifts," *Discovering Your Spiritual Gifts*, Number 1 (Berrien Springs, MI: Institute of Church Ministry, 1982).

CHAPTER 8

A Multi-million Dollar Enterprise

The folded chart is still in the possession of the senior author (Roger). Back in the early sixties, when he served as a conference superintendent of education, he traveled from church to church and preached about the values of a Christian education. He would whip out the now-faded chart and use the impressive data contained therein to clinch the final argument. It was hard to beat.

And what were the mysterious numbers? Of those who had completed all their education through college graduation in the Adventist school system, 88 percent had been baptized and were still members. For those with the same amount of education, but all outside Adventist schools, the figure was only 32 percent. For those who had completed academy with all twelve grades in Adventist schools, 72 percent were still around. Twelve years of public school could claim only 36 percent. The comparable figures for elementary graduates were 48 percent and 28 percent. Need more be said?

Yes! The chart contains no information as to where and when the data were collected. We know nothing about how representative the sample was of the Adventist population in general, how the information was secured, or what methodological safeguards may have been employed. And even if the study measured up to research respectability, today the data are very old—at least 30 years. The church desperately needs accurate, up-to-date, scientifically respectable data on the relationship between Adventist education and youth retention in the North American church.

Think for a moment of the immensity of the denomination's commitment to Christian education. "Beginning with the first elementary school in Battle Creek in 1872, the church's educational system has expanded into a huge international network—4,583 elementary, 643 secondary, and 84 tertiary programs. The church employs more than 40,000 teachers in its system."[1] The costs are mind-boggling. Truly, it is a multi-million dollar enterprise.

Of course, if our school system results in saving our youth for the kingdom and training them for the Master's service, it will be worth every penny it costs. No reasonable person could question the value of this mission field above all mission fields. But, as in any enterprise, accountability is required. Are our schools doing what they set out to do? Are they turning the little saintlets sent there into saints and putting them on an escalator to heaven? Do Adventist schools deliver "the goods"?

We cannot answer that question with any degree of finality until some years down the road, when we discover what decisions these teenagers—then adults—have made concerning their place in the church. But the survey did include a number of questions in the area of education. By relating these to key attitude statements, it is possible to gain some insights into the influence of Adventist schooling on church retention. To do this is the purpose of this chapter.

Educational Background

Only 23 percent of our sample never attended Seventh-day Adventist schools on the elementary level. On the other hand, about a third (34 percent) spent all eight years in church schools. The others were distributed quite evenly as follows: one year, 5 percent; two years, 6 percent; three years, 6 percent; four years,

6 percent; five years, 5 percent; six years, 6 percent; seven years, 9 percent.

At the time of the survey (1987-88 school year) about half were attending Seventh-day Adventist academies (30 percent day and 21 percent boarding). This agrees with other observations that about half of Adventist youth attend our schools. It also makes it possible to contrast the two groups on a number of attitudes and behaviors. Most of those who were not in Adventist schools were attending public high school (42 percent of the total) with 2 percent in other private schools, 3 percent in home study, and 1 percent not in school.

Since we often hear about students who do not want to attend Adventist schools but are coerced to do so by their parents, and since such situations could presumably affect attitudes, we asked our sample if they had ever been forced or persuaded to attend an Adventist school against their wishes. Only a minority (17 percent) said they had experienced such compulsion. The other 83 percent had exercised free choice. We compared the responses of the two groups on 10 key questions concerning attitudes toward religion and the church. Table 8-1 displays the results. The percentages represent those who agreed with each statement.

Note that those who were forced to attend Adventist schools were more negative on every item than those who were not. Probably, some students have learned to love a school, even though they didn't want to attend in the first place. But, overall, forcing seems to promote alienation.

Finally, we asked the teenagers what they intended to do after finishing the twelfth grade. Their responses were as follows: attend an Adventist college, 40 percent; attend a non-Adventist college, 20 percent; vocational training, 3 percent; go directly to work, 2 percent; enlist in the military, 4 percent; undecided, 31 percent.

Two points seem obvious. First, most Adventist teenagers do not intend to make high school the terminus of their education. Second, there is an ample area in which Adventist college

TABLE 8-1

Comparison of Attitudes Between TEENAGERS WHO WERE FORCED TO ATTEND ADVENTIST SCHOOLS AND THOSE WHO WERE NOT

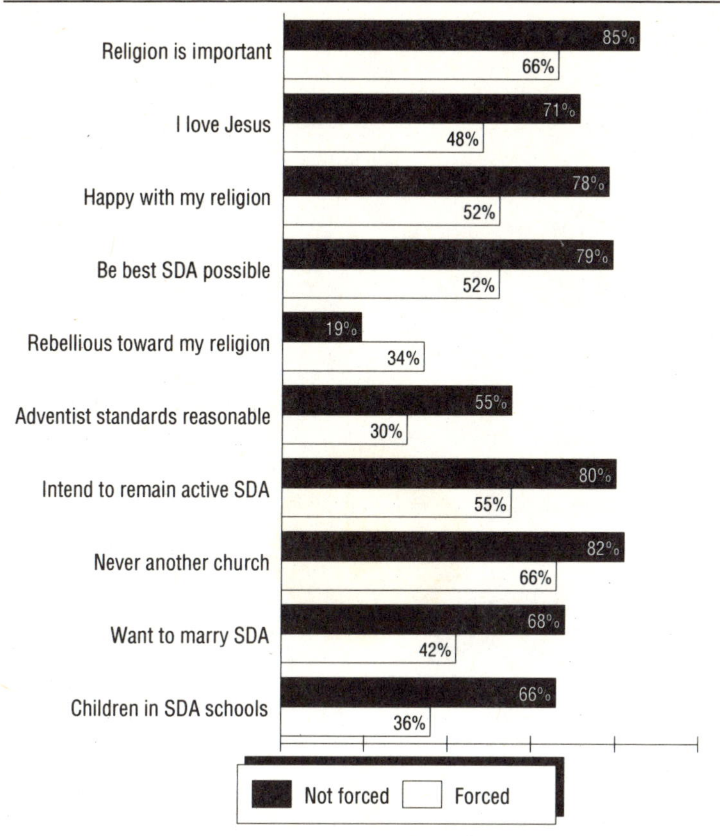

recruiters may work—persuading the 20 percent thinking of other colleges to switch, but especially among the nearly one third who are still undecided about future education.

Attitudes toward Schools and Teachers

Many studies (some cited in another chapter) have shown that the quality of relationships between the youth and those they perceive as spiritual authority figures impacts adolescent attitudes toward religion and thus behavior, such as leaving the church or remaining in it. Therefore, several of our questions explored these relationships.

We asked our respondents how close a relationship they had with Adventist teachers. Of those presently attending an Adventist academy, 40 percent said "very close" or "somewhat close," 38 percent said "only moderate," and 18 percent said "not close" or "distant." For the entire group the corresponding figures were 34 percent, 32 percent, and 17 percent. (Failure of these figures to total 100 percent is due to those who said the question did not apply to them.)

The importance of this concept is emphasized by our finding that there was a significant correlation between the closeness of the relationships that the teenagers perceived with significant others in their lives and the extent to which they expressed happiness with their religion. If youth are to have a joyous faith, *they must have happy relationships with some people within that faith*.

In response to the question, "To what extent have Adventist teachers aided you in growing toward independent adulthood?" 57 percent said "very supportive" or "usually favorable," 39 percent said "not much help," and 4 percent said "tried to hold me back." This is crucial in view of the fact that we found a significant relationship between perceived restraint and feelings of rebellion.

The chief developmental task of adolescence is to gain independence from adult authority figures and gain one's own sense of identity and autonomy. During this turbulent period, fighting for independence is as important as fighting for oxygen. Thus, teenagers who perceive restraint in the emancipation process are more likely to rebel against their religion.[2] It is our task to help them to achieve responsible adulthood and not to frustrate this development.

In the same vein we asked about the enforcement they had experienced from Adventist teachers. For those presently in academy, strict enforcement was perceived by 34 percent, moderate enforcement by 42 percent, and lenient enforcement by 17 percent. For the total group the comparable figures were 28 percent, 35 percent, and 16 percent. The remainder had not been under any Adventist teachers. Thus, the strict and moderate categories decrease, and the lenient remains essentially the same.

We were also interested in certain influences on spiritual experience. Teenagers were asked to rate several of these influences on a five-point scale from "most helpful" to "most unhelpful." For ease of comparison we have reduced these to simply "helpful" and "unhelpful," with the neutral group represented by the extent to which these two do not add to 100 percent.

Overall Group	Helpful	Unhelpful
What I learned at school	53%	18%
Members of my school family	33%	27%
My teachers' spiritual commitment	48%	17%

The above is challenging because it seems to indicate that the lives of the teachers in our schools are not fully congruent with the message we teach. In fairness, however, we point out that for those presently in academy, 58 percent found the spiritual commitment of the teachers helpful, and only 10 percent rated it unhelpful. Perhaps that is why some who once attended Adventist schools are no longer there. Only 39 percent of the group in public schools had found the spiritual commitment of their teachers to be a helpful influence on their own spiritual development.

And what about role models? "Are there any Adventists whom you admire so much that you would love to be 'just like' them, and whom you would feel terrible about if you heard that they left the church?" In our sample 32 percent put some teachers in that category. But the remaining 68 percent could not recall any teachers who would match that description.

This is unfortunate since we found significant correlations between the extent to which teenagers express admiration of adults who are important in their lives and both their desire to become the best Seventh-day Adventist Christians they can and their intention to remain Adventists when they are on their own. It can be concluded that youth imitate spiritual role models as they do other role models such as movie stars, sports celebrities, and musicians.

We also wanted to know how the teenagers felt about learning doctrines by various methods—one of which was school Bible classes. Nearly half (48 percent) felt the approach was "excellent" or "pretty good," 26 percent saw it as "OK," and 19 percent said "barely OK" or "can't stand." Of those presently in academy, 60 percent chose the most positive grouping. Among the total group, the preferred method for learning doctrines was "talking to someone I like"—rated by 69 percent as "excellent" or "pretty good." This points up once again the relational nature of adolescent religion.

Comparison of Academy and Public High Students

The teenagers were asked to respond to the same 10 attitudinal statements given above concerning religion, the church, and their future in it by use of a five-point scale ranging from "strongly agree" to "strongly disagree." These statements are key to the overall research purpose of studying retention in the church. In order to investigate the impact of Adventist education, we have contrasted in Table 8-2 the answers of the 773 academy students with those of the 634 youth attending public high. The percentages are obtained by combining the "somewhat agree" and the "strongly agree" categories.

TABLE 8-2

Comparison of Attitudes Between TEENAGERS WHO ATTEND ADVENTIST ACADEMIES AND THOSE WHO ATTEND PUBLIC SCHOOLS

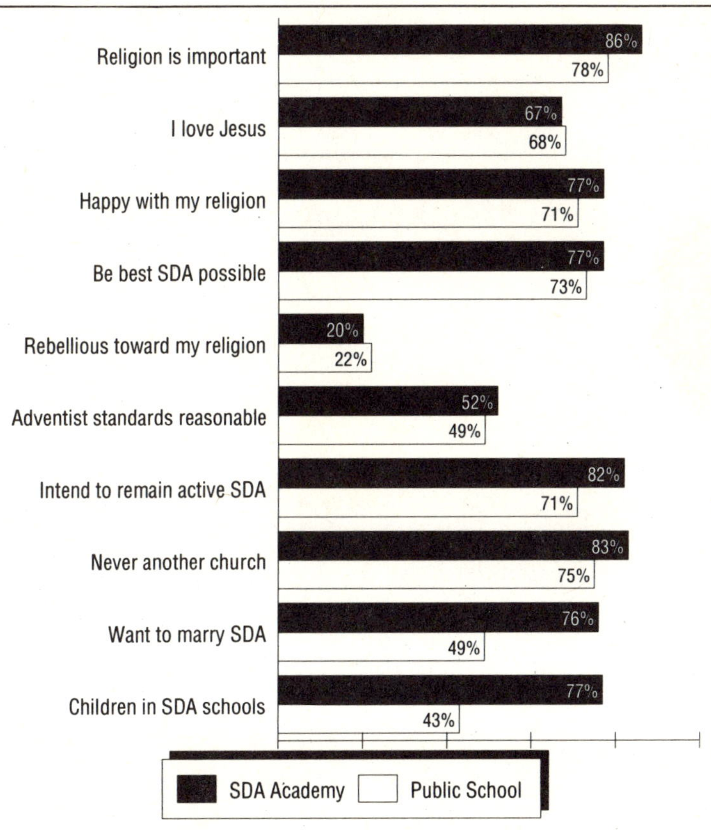

In every case but that of affirming a love experience with Jesus Christ, where the percentages are virtually equal, the academy students are more positive toward religion than those in public school are. But the differences are slight in areas such as rebellious feelings, Adventist standards, and being a good Christian. The differences are only moderate in importance of and happiness with religion.

The contrasts become greater in the area of a future relationship to Adventism, and the most dramatic differences concern marrying Adventists and sending one's children to Adventist schools. Even if those in academy do not view their present religious experience a great deal differently than those in public education do, they are much more likely to look to a future that preserves an Adventist way of life. Whether or not this future vision results in corresponding behavior, of course, remains to be seen in the coming years of the research project.

Whereas Table 8-2 compares students on the schools they are presently attending, we also correlated a number of variables with the number of years spent in Adventist schools. We found that those who have spent more years in Adventist education are more likely to want their own future children to attend Adventist schools. They also are somewhat more likely to express agreement with Adventist standards and to affirm their intentions to remain Adventists. They are not, however, any more likely than those who have gone to public schools to express happiness with their religion.

We might conclude that Adventist schooling produces belief in doctrine, faith in an underlying ideal, and resolutions for the future. It does not necessarily result in a more personally experienced religion. This is compatible with the research of Menegusso in Sao Paulo, Brazil, who found that long exposure to Adventist parochial education increased intellectual beliefs but lessened the experiential dimension.[3]

It also harmonizes with Noble's study of senior students in Adventist academies in the Pacific Northwest, which found that students believe less than they know and practice less than they believe.[4]

Certainly, one of the great challenges for our educators is to make Adventist education experiential. The Bible class members may memorize Luke 11:5, 6, but if they have never *experienced* the responsibility of needing some food to set before someone who is hungry, the principle has not been internalized. One cannot learn to swim by sitting on a sofa and reading a swimming manual. Likewise, religion requires laboratory time. When the bell that closes the lecture period rings, the lesson is but half taught.

Another set of questions had to do with feelings about Adventists. Again we contrasted academy with public high students. Table 8-3 displays this information.

TABLE 8-3

How Do You Feel About Adventists?
COMPARISONS BETWEEN ADVENTIST ACADEMY AND PUBLIC SCHOOL ATTENDERS

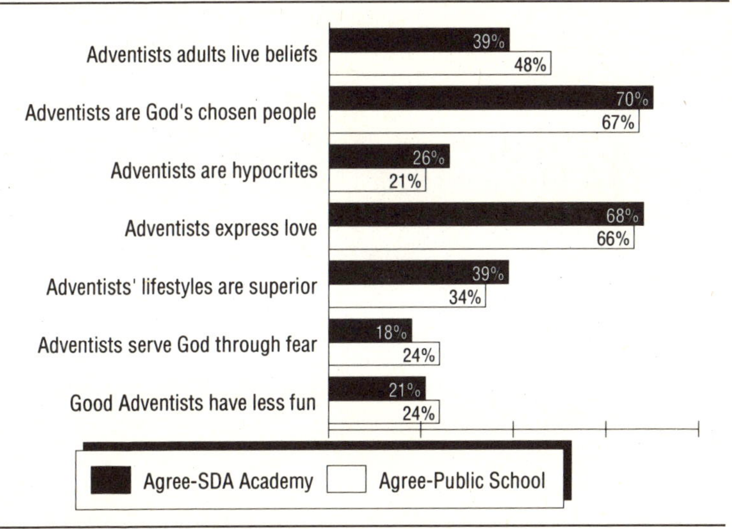

Those who attend academy are slightly more likely to believe that Adventists are a chosen people and that Adventist lifestyles are superior, and they are somewhat less likely to see fear as the motive for serving God. Each of these questions relates to correct *belief*. But they are not as likely to perceive Adventist adults as living up to what they believe and more likely to see them as hypocrites. This is the affective or feeling dimension of religion. The challenge of Adventist education remains not only to teach correct belief but also to help young people fall in love with Jesus Christ and His mission to the world.

Finally, our hearts go out to some who would like to attend a Christian school but have not found the way to make their dream a reality.

Note these comments: "I go to a public high school. I do not like attending this school since I am very uncomfortable there and it is changing me."

"I can't afford to go to a Christian academy as I did last year (I'm still paying off my bill). So now I have to go to a public school, and I know there are gonna be a lot of obstacles in my way tempting me, some that I will fail to pass, and it bothers me thinking about it."

"My parents couldn't pay the academy bill, and they, almost crying, had to take me out. I have been going to church schools all my life, and I wanted to finish in a church school."

"I would like to attend academy, but with my dad and five kids it's too expensive."

These are just a sample. As a church we have done a great deal with worthy student funds, but we need to do more. Would that we could put a Christian education within the grasp of every teenager who really wants it—another challenge to educational and financial leadership.

This chapter has offered some interesting gleanings about Adventist Christian education. As the succeeding years of research proceed, the information will grow in richness and ability to suggest positive solutions. Working together as educators, parents, pastors, and church leaders we may yet find ways to keep more of our precious youth within the fold and to train them for God's service.

References

[1] "Adventists and Higher Education," [Editorial Introduction], *Adventist Review*, March 2, 1989, p. 18.

[2] See Roger L. Dudley, *Why Teenagers Reject Religion and What to Do About It* (Washington, DC: Review and Herald Publishing Association, 1978), chapter 3.

[3] Eliseu N. Menegusso, "An Investigation of the Relationship Between Religiosity, Amount of Exposure to Seventh-day Adventist Parochial Education and Other Selected Variables" (Ed.D. Dissertation, Andrews University, 1980).

[4] Joel N. Noble, "Certain Religious and Educational Attitudes of Senior High School Students in Seventh-day Adventist Schools in the Pacific Northwest," (Ph.D. Dissertation, University of Oregon, 1971).

CHAPTER 9

Fallout From the Rat Race

Imagine, if you will, the following true scene from a large Adventist church school.

A fund-raising contest was under way with a Schwinn bicycle offered by the promoting company as the grand prize. Selling their products, the students hustled from door to door in their neighborhoods. One financially secure grandmother of a student took keen interest in who was leading the pack of superstar sellers. Repeatedly she would buy five of an item from her grandson, make the check out to the religious school organization (saving the receipt for a charitable tax deduction), and store the items for her next garage sale.

On the day the contest closed, she instructed her grandson, "Call me a half hour before the contest ends, and tell me who is the highest and by how much." The competitiveness was now augmented by a sense of good business—it would surely be worth up to another $20 to secure a new bicycle.

Hardly a dress rehearsal for heaven, is it? As the incident unfolded, how could the labor of the faithful teachers—whose gospel message included: others first, the Great Commandment, and the Golden Rule—not be neutralized by this me-first, money-is-power, competitive spirit? Those students whose sales had resulted from honest door-knocking and who had lost—not so fair-and-square—were appalled and disillusioned.

When the commercial entrepreneur had ventured into the school with such a surefire fund raiser, the unsuspecting principal had perceived the convenience of the arrangement—letting an outside party handle the work and promotion—and did not foresee the results. Nevertheless, such a situation would not have invaded the spiritual climate of his school had he previously decided what types of motivation would be allowed. It is understood that in a climate of competition individuals will all work *against* one another.

How Youth Are Faring

Perhaps the above incident is (hopefully) an isolated one. But how much competition *do* students in the Adventist system perceive? And how do they feel about it? With unparalleled curiosity we analyzed the responses of what our young people had to say about competition. Here is their overall perspective:

I can hardly stand it	4%
There's way too much	8%
I can handle it, but I don't like it	46%
I'm able to ignore it	22%
I sort of like it	15%
I thrive on it	5%

The competitive system appears to be reinforcing *very well* the self-esteem of about one teenager in 20. Another three out of 20 were willing to say that it works for them enough of the time that they feel they are winning more than they are losing by it. Although winning is not a shoo-in experience for them as for the thrivers, they are challenged by it, and it is rewarding when they are occasionally successful. Combining these two categories, we find that about one in five found competition agreeable to them.

A few more, 22 percent as compared to 20 percent, handled

the situation by denial—they were able to ignore it. It might be hypothesized that the people in this group are on the fringes of the winning group and have enough positive perceptions about themselves that they can pretend this category of affirmation doesn't matter. They are not really on the "outside, looking in," because they've indicated they're not looking; they are ignoring.

Then we come to the largest group, 46 percent, nearly half of the respondents. Translated into numbers, this means that 695 teenagers in this one study alone felt this way: "I can handle it, but I don't like it." In other words, they are coping with it, and even adjusting, but wish they didn't have to play dog-eat-dog.

The last 12 percent were wholly discouraged by competition. Of these, 4 percent can hardly stand it. Just 4 percent may sound insignificant, but this translates into 60 teenagers from just this one study. In order to have 5 percent creaming off the competition benefits at the top, we have 4 percent at the other end being made miserable by the system.

A Philosophical Junction

Before we examine what teenagers perceive to be the sources of this competition, let us first deal with a philosophical question. Many at this point will say, as did the principal of a parochial junior high school who was asked why he allowed such fierce competition to exist under his jurisdiction, "Well, that's the way it will be when they get to the academy across the way, and they might as well get used to it." Of course the academy principal's response was, "That's what we have to prepare them to face in the real world."

Here we have come to a philosophical junction. What is the purpose of our Christian education—to prepare young people for the real world or for the real heaven? And if the young person is not able to find emotional safety within the religious community, where will it be found at all? Is there no haven of love to which one can escape and bask in brotherly/sisterly love? If we provide a little "heaven on earth" for teenagers instead of the cut-throat competition of the society around us, will they not find the gospel attracting them like a magnet? With these challenging questions before us, let us explore the origins of this stressful system.

Sources of Competition

Teenagers perceived the undesirable aspects of competition to be stimulated by the following sources:

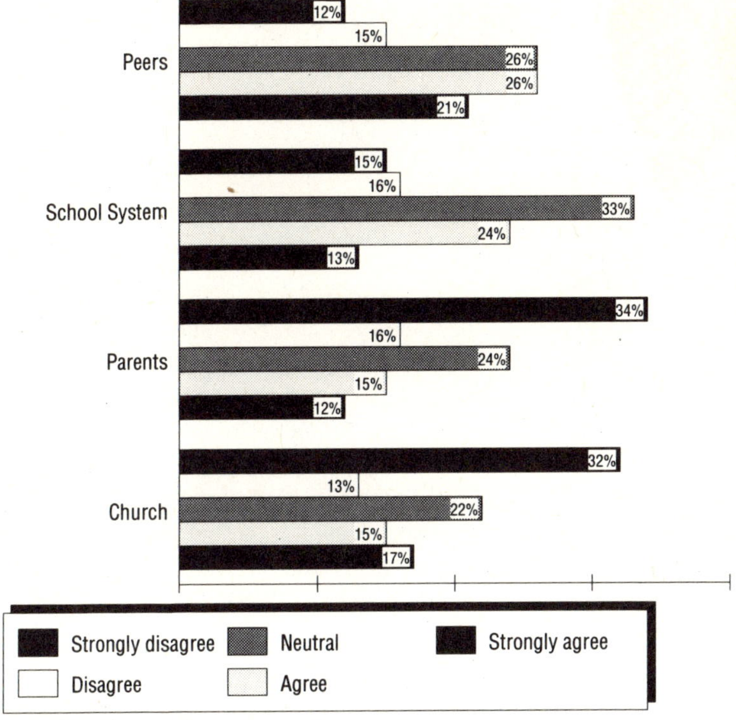

If the two categories "strongly agree" and "agree" are combined in the peer category, the result is that a whopping 47 percent of the teenagers perceived their peers as a stimulus for undesirable competition. This is understandable since age mates are the object of the competition.

The accusing finger was pointed at areas of church and school as well. When we combine the two "agree" categories and the two "disagree" categories, the results, in descending order of agreement, are:

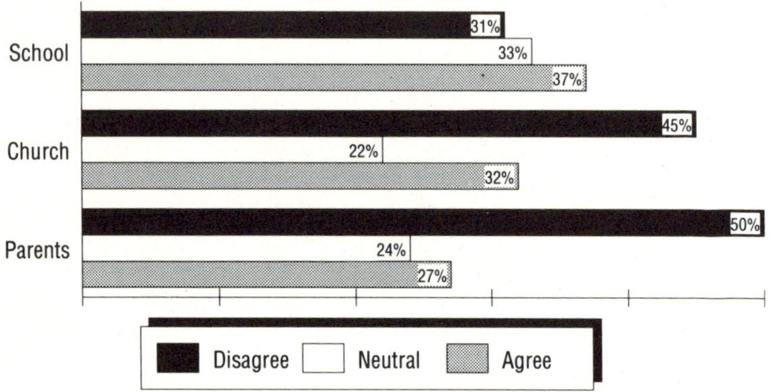

Of the three institutions—home, church, and school—teenagers perceived their parents as the least source of competitive pressure. The response they rated was: "My parents, who compare me with others or push me to be No. 1." Approximately one-fourth of the teenagers studied agreed that their parents fit this description.

The church and school, as denominational institutions, are more subject to influence from denominational leaders and policies than are peers and parents. Thus it behooves us to examine the church and school sources of competition, which might be more subject to modification and which, in turn, might reduce the competitive pressures from peers and parents.

The teenagers' perceptions of school and church were not far apart in the category of *agreement*; 37 percent and 32 percent, respectively, agreed that these are sources of competition. But 45 percent *dis*agreed that the church is a source of competition, whereas only 31 percent disagreed in regard to the school. The school, then, seems to have an edge over the church in being perceived by teenagers as the source of competitive activities.

Most who volunteered free responses about competition within the church mentioned that the adults go to church to show off their clothes, see who contributes the most money, and flaunt status symbols rather than to really worship the Lord.

The school, in addition to ranking higher than church and parents as a fountain of competition, is also where the most time is spent with peers, the actual highest source. Let us, then, consider the school. A summary of the competitive activities in one seventh- and eighth-grade setting included: annual science fair contest, annual spelling bee championship, courtesy king and queen contest, first chair in band, best choir member, John Philip Sousa award, class officers, selling contests, honor roll, sports captains, class fund-raising contests, and JMV officers.

What began as class night fun for high school graduations has dipped as low as eighth-grade graduations in choosing best dressed, most likely to succeed, most humorous, best liked, best all-around person, most talented, among others. Now it seems that there would be enough honors to go around with such a long list. That realization makes it all the more devastating when some get *nothing* after the achievers, excellers, and glory-grabbers have skimmed off the lion's share of the rewards.

How does a young person survive all this? As one thoughtful girl articulated: "My best friend is also my potential enemy in practically everything that comes up." Seventh- and eighth-graders are roughly 12 and 13 years old—in early adolescence when self-esteem is formative, not normative. By the time they have reached mid-teens, how has their developmental unreadiness to cope with competition affected their outlook on the church?

Effects on Attitudes

The undesirable aspects of competition ranked sixth in the 27 influences on intentions to remain Adventists tested by statistical procedures (see chapter 10). The only indicators that ranked higher were the degree of agreement with standards, the frequency of personal prayers, perceived love expressed by church members, the frequency of church attendance, and the degree to which teenagers perceive that the church meets their spiritual needs.

The teenagers have spoken. Clearly, their attitudes toward remaining in the church are influenced by their dislike for the competition experienced there. This is a paradox in light of the swelling move for denominational interschool sports by college students, who are but a few years older than the teenagers in this study. A serious question to consider is whether the earlier attitudinal correlation between competition and church attrition is still operating.

Competition in Sports

A poem by John Martin reveals the extremes to which even adults, not just youth, become involved in winning at sports. Martin's poem describes a baseball game. A small boy stands at bat, and the bases are loaded. It is up to the lad to hit the winning run. The pitcher winds up and throws the ball. The little boy swings . . . and misses. The most memorable lines of the poem come next. They tell of an adult who shouts, "Strike out the bum!" Tears fill the child's eyes. The games has lost its fun. Martin appeals to us to recognize that the lad is not a man yet, but just a child standing all by himself, with a lot of responsibility falling upon him.

When this poem was read in an office setting, one secretary remarked, "I can't believe adults would treat a child that way."

A worker across the hall overheard her and stepped out of his office. "Oh yes, they do," he said. "I coach a Little League baseball team, and I can tell you that the grown-ups act like that all the time. Where there's cheering, there is also booing. My worst problem is keeping the adults in line."

The coach was then asked why he thought the adults would do such a thing. His thoughtful response was that perhaps the adults are venting their own aggressions and hostilities through sports, which appears to be an acceptable way to let such emotions fly—even if it happens to be a children's game.

Now if the competitive intensity of even adults can overpower their commonsense compassion toward little players, what chance do young athletes have of controlling their emotions during a hot contest? And how will *they* react to the pressure?

We do not intend to take a position on what seems to be the most current competitive concern among Adventists—interschool sports.[1] This is a very complicated issue, with fine nuances interpreted to support both sides. Our study did not specifically address the sports issue, and, after all, neither of us has distinguished himself/herself by prowess in athletics so we will leave this to the experts. Frankly, we have some difficulty differentiating between the results of intramural games (allowed by both sides) and interschool games (in dispute). It seems that *how* you play is more important than *whom* you play. But whether that means that both types ought to be permitted or that both types ought to be banned, we will leave to wiser heads to decide.

Still, we hope those wiser heads will take a close look at what competition is doing to the spiritual lives of their students. One of us (Roger) once served as principal of a boarding academy. Upon taking up his duties, he learned that the previous year his school and another academy had played a big basketball game. His academy had won.

It soon became apparent that students at the sister school were gearing up for a return match and the revenge they felt quite sure such a contest would provide. At a joint Bible conference a student leader from the other academy jumped up on a table and challenged Roger's school, making it very clear what he felt the humiliating outcome would be. After observing the verbal exchanges between representatives of the two schools, Roger felt he had but one option—to cancel the scheduled game.

It was not a popular decision. Many students at his own

school did not understand, and the students from the other academy were livid. They sent him letters stating that his school was too cowardly to play because its faculty and students knew what a thrashing they would take. He was afraid, but not of losing (which really made no difference). Rather he was afraid of the spirit of rivalry, dominance, and outright hatred.

However we settle the matter of sports, we must resist that which will destroy Christian love and concern.

A Few Suggestions

We would not want to leave the impression that the athletic program is the sole offender, or even the primary one, in engendering a competitive spirit. Probably, athletics have been given too great a share of the blame whenever competition is discussed. We have noted a number of other areas in home, school, and church that promote rivalry rather than cooperation. We are concerned from a theological standpoint that such a spirit is not in harmony with the self-sacrificing servanthood taught and modeled by our Lord. In the three and one-half years that Jesus schooled His disciples, the most important lesson that He taught them was "how not to compete."[2] And we are concerned from an empirical perspective for our teenagers have told us, regardless of appearances to the contrary, that the stress of having to compete is difficult to live with and damaging to the self-esteem and Christian experience.

Now we are not suggesting that schools get rid of grades, honor rolls, friendly ball games, awards, or contests. Nor do we expect churches to drop Ingathering goals, elective offices, or fund drives. These motivators have useful purposes. But it does seem that our leaders—especially of youth—ought to pay a great deal of attention to how these things are presented and the manner in which they are implemented.

For example, we must be sure that no one is ever made to feel like a loser and of less worth as a human being because he or she does not have the same amount of specific ability as someone else. We must never allow any youth to be humiliated or demeaned. This means that a competence, talent, or spiritual gift must be developed in *every* young person—else the individual self-worth will be lowered merely in being passed over the many times when excellence is sought, even when the selections for superiority are conducted in a Christlike manner.

We must constantly emphasize that God accepts us not on the basis of our performance but on the basis of Jesus' performance. While we should encourage every young person to excel to the utmost of his or her abilities in any field, we must make clear that every human being is of infinite value because of creation in God's image and redemption through the costly sacrifice of Jesus Christ.

We also believe that one of the supreme objectives for youth groups, whatever the locale, is to build a sense of community. We should learn to cooperate in common purposes rather than to compete against each other. We should assist rather than frustrate each other in reaching for personal goals. The strong should aid the weak, and the brilliant should help the struggler. "By all that has given us advantage over another—be it education and refinement, nobility of character, Christian training, religious experience—we are in debt to those less favored; and, so far as lies in our power, we are to minister unto them. If we are strong, we are to stay up the hands of the weak."[3]

We constitute a Christian family where "each of you should look not only to your own interests, but also to the interests of others" (Philippians 2:4). We have achieved our finest Christian hour when we desire to build others rather than to beat them.

Is this too idealistic for "the real world"? Not for those who are bound for the real heaven.

References

[1] See *Adventist Review*, October 13, 1988, pp. 10-15, with Introduction by Myron Widmer, "Yes," by Walt Hamerslough, and "No," by Jim Roy.

[2] *Ibid.*, p. 12.

[3] Ellen G. White, *The Desire of Ages* (Mountain View, CA: Pacific Press Publishing Association, 1940), p. 440.

CHAPTER 10

Call Person to Person

I can see Christ distinctly in some of the people that have the same religion, and I pray that someday other people will be able to say that about me."

"I know that it sounds as if I'm losing faith in the church. I'm not. It's the people within the church."

Ah! People! People who need people are the luckiest people in the world. In the final analysis it's not the doctrines, or the buildings, or the organization, or the program that determines whether a youth commits to Christ and His church. It's the people.

"Teens determine what's true based on what they experience in relationships," wrote Dann Spader of Moody Bible Institute in 1984. "If you want to influence a teenager, you've got to establish a relationship with him."[1]

"Youth want to worship the God who sits next to them in people," Merton Strommen, a Lutheran, had observed earlier in 1973.[2]

He . . . Made the Two One

Leaders such as Bruce Larson in the church renewal movement[3] have added a new phrase to our ecclesiastical vocabulary: "relational theology." A good case can be made that the heart of all true religion is a matter of relationships—first with God, then with our own inner selves, and finally with others in our life spaces and with our environment.

When Jesus was asked for the greatest commandment, He gave a relational answer: Love God with all . . . Love your neighbor (Matt. 22:37-39). And the essence of all sin is the breaking of relationships for "everything that does not come from faith is sin" (Rom. 14:23). Recovery from sin begins in a restoration of relationships.

For Larson the key ingredients of Christ's love are summed up in the words *affirmation* and *vulnerability*.[4] To open up our own lives and become vulnerable to a teenager is to begin an authentic relationship. And to affirm, or recognize, the worth (though hidden to others) of the youth is to move the relationship Godward. As the adult becomes a model of one-in-relationship, the adolescent is warmed and led to a lasting relationship with the heavenly Friend.

These observations seem to indicate that teenagers evaluate their religion not by soundness of theology or correctness of fact but by *feelings*. Is it true that the Christian teenager's social heart overrules the head in spiritual perceptions?

Apparently so. Strommen's research found that the best indicator of how young people view their church is the degree to which they feel they belong among, and can identify with, the people they picture as the church. Indeed, the best predictor of which young people will be disappointed in their church is the feelings they have about how well they fit in with groups in their congregations.[5]

Likewise, Warren Hartman reported that among Methodist dropouts whom he had contacted, the most frequent response given for their attrition from their church was failure to feel accepted, loved, and wanted.[6]

Frederick Whitam, who studied the retention of young people who committed themselves in a Billy Graham Crusade in New York City, concluded that interpersonal factors—rather than formal ideological commitment to Graham's cause—were the important determinants of retention on the part of the evangelist's youthful followers.[7]

Our study confirmed that the same is true among Adventist youth. When those variables that predict the teenagers' intentions to remain Adventists were ranked by a statistical technique known as stepwise multiple regression, the 12 items that contributed significantly to the prediction were as follows:

1. Agreement with rules/standards
2. Frequency of personal prayer
3. Love expressed by Adventist members
4. Frequency of church attendance
5. Church meeting spiritual needs
6. Agreement on the undesirable effects of competition
7. Aid felt toward gaining independence
8. Both parents are members of the church
9. Frequency of Bible reading
10. Perceived spiritual commitment of parents
11. Closeness of relationships
12. Perception that members live what they believe

While agreement with the rules and standards of the church was ranked first (chapter 6 was devoted to this crucial subject), a number of the others are relational in nature. A relationship with God is foundational to all relationships, and this is reflected in numbers 2, 5, and 9. But several others deal with the horizontal relationships with God's people. Notice that the third highest factor was *love expressed by members*. Youth who sense they are members of a loving, caring community are more likely to choose to remain in such fellowship.

After all, alienation from the church and religion is rarely a doctrinal matter. A national study of Adventist academy students showed that on a scale to measure belief in fundamental Adventist doctrines with a possible range of 9 to 45, the average score was 41. If the students had been normally distributed between belief and unbelief, a mean score of 27 would have been expected. The mean of 41—only four points below the maximum possible—reveals a very strong intellectual acceptance of Adventist beliefs. Yet the study found that about half of these youth were alienated from at least some aspects of their religion.[8]

Item 7 can be important as the teens perceive significant adults in their lives (mothers, fathers, Adventist teachers, church leaders, Sabbath school teachers) as aiding or hindering them in the primary task of adolescence—growing toward independent adulthood. If we are not there for them during this tough and crucial task, they may conclude that they don't need us anywhere—or our religion either.

The 11th influence was *closeness of relationships*. How teenagers see the interactions with important people in their lives on a continuum from very close to distant makes a real difference in the decisions they are making about their future with the church. Now, 11th place might not appear so high on a list ending with 12. However, 27 variables in all were tested, and the 12 appearing on the table, at which point the computer ended its calculations, all ranked higher than the following 15: frequency of church attendance by parents, attendance at Adventist schools, self-perception of class rank, degree of enforcement experienced throughout life, influence of home instruction, influence of home members, influence of school instruction, influence of school family, perceived spiritual commitment of teachers, influence of church members, perceived spiritual commitment of pastors, social needs met by church, talking doctrines over with someone liked, and family worship.

Other tests agreed. It was found that adolescents who perceive close relationships with significant others express more happiness with their religion and that adolescents who admire significant adults express greater desire to become the best Seventh-day Adventist Christians possible.

Who Then Is Important?

The critical question then is, *Who* is important to the teenagers? Again, let us examine previous studies and then see whether the findings on Adventist youth agree.

The critical importance of who the significant others are is borne out in two comparative studies on ecumenical youth by Kevin Treston and Raymond Whiteman.[9]

Whiteman, who studied the subjects' interpersonal relations and the type of religious education experienced by them, found that the basic belief system developed by a child in the family remained and that the attitude toward parents, based on early emotions and fears, resulted in the child's filial attitudes toward God.

Treston's study found the importance of parents and home relations a constant factor in the religious development of the child. Children who mirrored adults possessed a higher degree of awareness of God, participated more in religious worship, and felt closer to God.

Samuel Morgan found that Catholic parents strongly influenced the frequency of their adolescent children's prayers by their own patterns. Data analyzed 11 years apart revealed declining frequency of prayers among daughters whose mothers prayed less and a somewhat lesser decline between fathers and sons.[10]

In an interdenominational study of Catholics, Southern Baptists, and Methodists, Hoge and Petrillo found that the Baptist youth revealed the most church commitment. An evaluation found that the Baptists practiced higher parental participation in church organization and engaged in more parental talk with the youth about church and religion.[11]

Another interdenominational study, of youth who attended Wesleyan, United Methodist, and American Baptist churches, by Robert Laurent revealed that quality relationships with both parents and pastors were important predictors of alienation from religion.[12]

The teenagers in our sample, as we reported in the chapter on the home, were asked to rate various influences on their spiritual experience. The members of the home family were rated somewhat helpful or most helpful by 74 percent. Comparable figures for members of the church family and members of the school family were 55 percent and 35 percent respectively. Although these figures give priority to the home, they also point to the critical nature of human relationships in all three arenas.

Youth are developing spiritually because they are in touch with other live, warm, caring human beings. It would not be stretching it too far to suggest that youth are also withering spiritually for lack of such flesh-and-blood connections.

We asked our adolescents how close a relationship they had with various classes of people. Percentages who chose somewhat close or very close were given in the chapter on the home. You may remember that four of the five highest positions are held by family members. The ranking of each category appears to be directly proportionate to the individuals with whom the teenagers spend the most time.

But something else is interesting. We have already mentioned that teenagers who perceived close relationships with significant others across the board were more likely to express happiness with their religion. But close relationships with church leaders and Sabbath school teachers were even more strongly predictive of happiness with religion than was the overall category. While not nearly as many youth are likely to feel as close to these two groups as they are to family members and peers, those who do are considerably more likely to be satisfied with their religious experience. What a challenge that presents to church leaders and Sabbath school teachers.

Parents, Take Heart

Any close relationship must be built on, at the very least, respect. Two people in real relationship learn to trust each other and believe in mutual sincerity and good will. They find something to *admire* in each other. Thus asking the teenagers what Adventists they admire so much that they would love to be "just like" them is to probe for relationships so potentially powerful that they could be decisive in holding a young person for Christ and His church.

The rankings are given in the chapter on the home, and, as might be expected, parents head the list. But the surprise is that after the parents, there is a reversal of adults and age-mates. Peers and siblings descend, while pastors and teachers ascend. Grandparents and adult members also rank higher than age-mates now.

Peers do not then appear to be the religious role models teenagers admire, in spite of adaptations they make to peer pressure. They may absorb some behaviors from those to whom they are close in age, but in reality they are looking to *adults* to chart the course of their religion. In their transition from child-principled morality to adult-principled morality, the teenagers are studying the values of the adults. Parents (and other adults), take courage! You have an opportunity to construct relationships that can introduce a youth to the heavenly Friend.

Adults, Take Caution

The sad part is that the religious role models they admire most, other than their parents, are not the same individuals to whom they feel closest. If these adults could only spend time nurturing relationships (and remember, the most important influence on teenagers' spiritual perceptions is the quality of relationships), think of the spiritual influence they could shed on these youth.

Perhaps part of the problem lies in the fact that busy adults are relieved when the teenagers entertain each other. But those who occupy their time also influence their behavior—something one of us (Janet) learned from parakeets.

She had always loved little parakeets that "talked." A

friend's parakeet knew that it could draw her from anywhere in the house over to its cage if it cocked its adorable little blue head and chattered, "And Jesus loves *meee*, too!"

She set about to get one of these fluffy charmers and began by buying books on training parakeets and inquiring of those who had successfully taught their birds to talk. One principle consistently came through. Don't have any other birds around, or they will communicate only with each other and ignore you.

And then the light dawned. When the bird is cut off from its own kind—socially starved, if you will—it will adjust to what is available—humans. These darling little creatures will mimic us in an attempt to communicate with *some*thing, even though they do not understand the meaning of the sounds they are making. Once Janet realized this, she forfeited the hours of pleasure a talking bird would provide for *two* birds that would sing instead.

You have likely reasoned the point. When we parents and significant adults do not spend *time* with our young people in meaningful dialogue or activities, are we actually starving their social natures into finding companionship elsewhere?

In General Conference worship one morning, Floyd Bresee was impressing the staff that time is love by the following illustration. A man's son sat alone on the front porch steps, slamming his baseball from his right hand into his gloved left hand. Dad hurried out the door, tussled him on the head, and said, "I love you, son," as he left.

"I don't want you to love me," the boy called after him. "I want you to play ball with me."

Enough said.

Closeness *and* Respect

Take note, however, that a close relationship between adult and young person is not enough. Without the element of respect present, the young person may enjoy the adult's company and even be influenced—but not in a positive vein. Remember, the age-mates are close, but do not necessarily look to each other for role models. The spiritual influencing of a teenager requires both closeness *and* respect. Neither alone will do.

This combination is supported by Michael Mason's research on Presbyterian youth. Mason found that actively religious youth "had had or were continuing to have a significant interaction with an adult for whom faith was an important aspect of life and who influenced them to continue to seek answers to their own faith questions."[13]

Notice that the finding does not end with "significant interaction with an adult" but continues with "for whom faith was an important aspect of life." Mason also found that all but one of these youth mentioned a significant adult *by name*! He concluded that viable and approachable role models might be considered the single most important factor as to whether or not a young person might grow toward a developed faith.

According to Patrick Moffett, when a teenager distinguishes such a person as a *significant other* in his or her life, there begins a distinct period of working for the approval of that adult. Immature adults, he found, not only blocked this transition from child-principled morality to adult-principled morality but even made some adolescents immune to the influence of instruction and materials that stimulate principled thinking.[14]

In summary, adolescents need to be shown the Christian life by a spiritual model as well as to be told. And this, in addition to giving them a pattern to follow, also provides a dim projection of what God must be like.

Also, adolescents need approval, but the approval is important only if they first value the approver as significant. Since teenagers tend to idealize, they seek the approbation of those whose Christian lives they have already examined and found attractive. The esteem of such persons they will solicit, perhaps subtly. Such adults are then in a position to influence the teenagers spiritually.

References

[1] Dann Spader, "Tired of Band-Aid Approaches to Youth Work?" *Moody Monthly*, January 1984, pp. 52-56.

[2] Merton P. Strommen, *Bridging the Gap* (Minneapolis: Augsburg Publishing House, 1973), pp. 64, 65.

[3] Bruce Larson, *No Longer Strangers* (Waco, TX: Word Books, 1971).

[4] *Ibid.*, p. 48.

[5] Merton P. Strommen, Milo L. Brekke, Ralph C. Underwager, and Arthur L. Johnson, *A Study of Generations* (Minneapolis: Augsburg, 1972), pp. 301, 295.

[6] Warren J. Hartman, *Membership Trends: A Study of Decline and Growth in the United Methodist Church 1949-1975* (Nashville: Discipleship Resources, 1976).

[7] Frederic L. Whitam, "Peers, Parents, and Christ: Interpersonal Influence in Retention of Teen-age Decisions Made at a Billy Graham Crusade," *Proceedings of the Southwestern Sociological Association* 19 (1968): pp. 154-158.

[8] Roger L. Dudley, "Selected Variables Related to Alienation from Religion as Perceived by Students Attending Seventh-day Adventist Academies in the United States" (Ed.D. dissertation, Andrews University, 1977): pp. 65-70.

[9] Kevin Treston, Raymond G. Whiteman, and Jerry G. Florent, "Catholic School Religious Training Versus Adolescent Background and Orientation: Two Comparative Studies," *Notre Dame Journal of Education* 6 (Spring 1975): pp. 59-64.

[10] Samuel Philip Morgan, "The Intergenerational Transmission of Religious Behavior: The Effect of Parents on Their Children's Frequency of Prayer" (Ph.D. dissertation, University of Arizona, 1980).

[11] Dean R. Hoge and Gregory H. Petrillo, "Determinants of Church Participation and Attitude Among High School Youth," *Journal for the Scientific Study of Religion* 17 (December 1978): pp. 359-379.

[12] C. Robert Laurent, "Selected Variables Related to Alienation From Religion Among Church-related High School Students" (Ph.D. dissertation, Andrews University, 1986).

[13] Michael M. Mason, "Faith Development of Young People: A Study of the Differences of Faith Development Among Youth Active in Church Programs and Those Who Have Dropped Out" (D.Min. dissertation, San Francisco Theological Seminary, 1984), abstract.

[14] Patrick S. Moffett, "The Preconventional Teen: A Study in Moral Development," *Journal of Pastoral Counseling* 16 (Fall-Winter 1981), pp. 53-60.

CHAPTER 11

One-on-One With God

The most important thing in life to me is Jesus and having a daily walk with Him. That is also my biggest struggle. I find it is too easy to wake up late and dash out the door without having morning worship. It is my toughest struggle.''

''I also feel continually learning more about God is very important, and I try to do as much of this as I can.''

The bottom line in all our youth work is to lead the young people into a personal relationship with God. The two young people in our sample, quoted above, capture something of the desire for companionship with the Divine. But we can also sense a note of frustration. Keeping the pipeline to Heaven open is not easy. Close relationships depend on time together, and in the hustle-bustle of modern life, it is easy to let that time get squeezed out.

Do personal devotions with the word of God still have power to shape adolescent lives? David Wilkerson tells how in a gang-dominated area of Harlem a social worker told him that giving these people religion was no answer to their problems; what they needed was better housing, more money and jobs, and a change of environment. Wilkerson felt discouraged and wondered why he had come to New York. Could his team ever really make a dent in those slums? But then a dark-haired girl named Rosa told him about her experience.

"One of your ladies gave me a little black book. She asked me to read it. I laughed at her, too, when she said Jesus would give me power over sin. But that night I started to read this little book that says on the cover, *San Juan*. I like this name 'John.' I read two chapters. I read how Jesus made water into wine, and I asked Him if He could change my heart.

"Mr. Wilkerson, something happened that night. Ever since, this block has been different. The piles of garbage still smell just as bad, the roaches in our apartments are just as thick, but in some way everything has changed. I have something inside me now that tells me God is with me, and He will be with me anywhere. I have many problems, but Jesus has changed the biggest problem of all. He has shown me how to live with myself."*

Now few, if any, of the teenagers in our study live in the slums or run with gangs. But their need for God is not one whit less. And this need can be supplied only as they experience a life-changing encounter with Jesus Christ (being born again) and as they then build and strengthen their relationship with Him through an active devotional life. After a brief description of the conversion backgrounds of our adolescents, we will examine their devotional behaviors.

Conversion Backgrounds

We asked our adolescents to describe their spiritual experience in terms of whether they had undergone a conversion that they could pinpoint in time as opposed to a gradually developing Christian consciousness. While 30 percent answered, "I've been a 'growing' Christian since I was young," and 15 percent checked, "I had a 'conversion' experience to Christ during a specific period," the remaining 55 percent said that it was probably a degree of both.

The proportions of the first two responses and the fuzziness of the third suggest that the dramatic, Paul-on-the-road-to-Damascus conversion is relatively rare in this group. The following facts reveal that these second-generation Adventists have identified with the church through the medium of their parents. In all but 4 percent of the cases, the mother was or had been a baptized member of the Adventist church. In 64 percent of the subjects, the mother was baptized before the birth of the teenager; in 13 percent, between birth and 6 years of age; and in 13 percent, between 7 and 12 years. Only 6 percent of the sample were teenagers when their mothers joined the church. For fathers the figure is 4 percent. Whatever direction they take in the future, these adolescents have come out of childhood wearing their parents' religion.

Now, facing independent adulthood, they must decide what to do about this inherited religion. Some have found a personal encounter with Christ. Others have decided to reject the faith of their parents. The majority are not yet sure. We may be able to help them with this momentous decision.

Teens and Time for God

We have suggested that encouraging the devotional life may be a fruitful approach. We asked our young people to tell us the frequency with which they engaged in 10 devotional or Christian lifestyle practices. The results are shown in Table 11-1.

We have dedicated a special chapter on family worship (chapter 3) to the first item, and have discussed witnessing in chapter 7. Here we confine ourselves to the middle eight.

Personal prayer comes out the best with 63 percent claiming to pray on a daily basis and another 16 percent praying at least weekly, for a total of 79 percent. Only 4 percent say they never pray. While this is encouraging, it must be remembered that the nature of the prayer occasions was not specified. Saying grace before meals, sending up a cry for help before the teacher distributes the exams, or murmuring "Now I lay me down to sleep" just before dozing off could all count. How much of this

TABLE 11-1

HOW OFTEN DO YOU PARTICIPATE IN THESE EXPERIENCES? PERSONAL CHRISTIAN LIFESTYLE

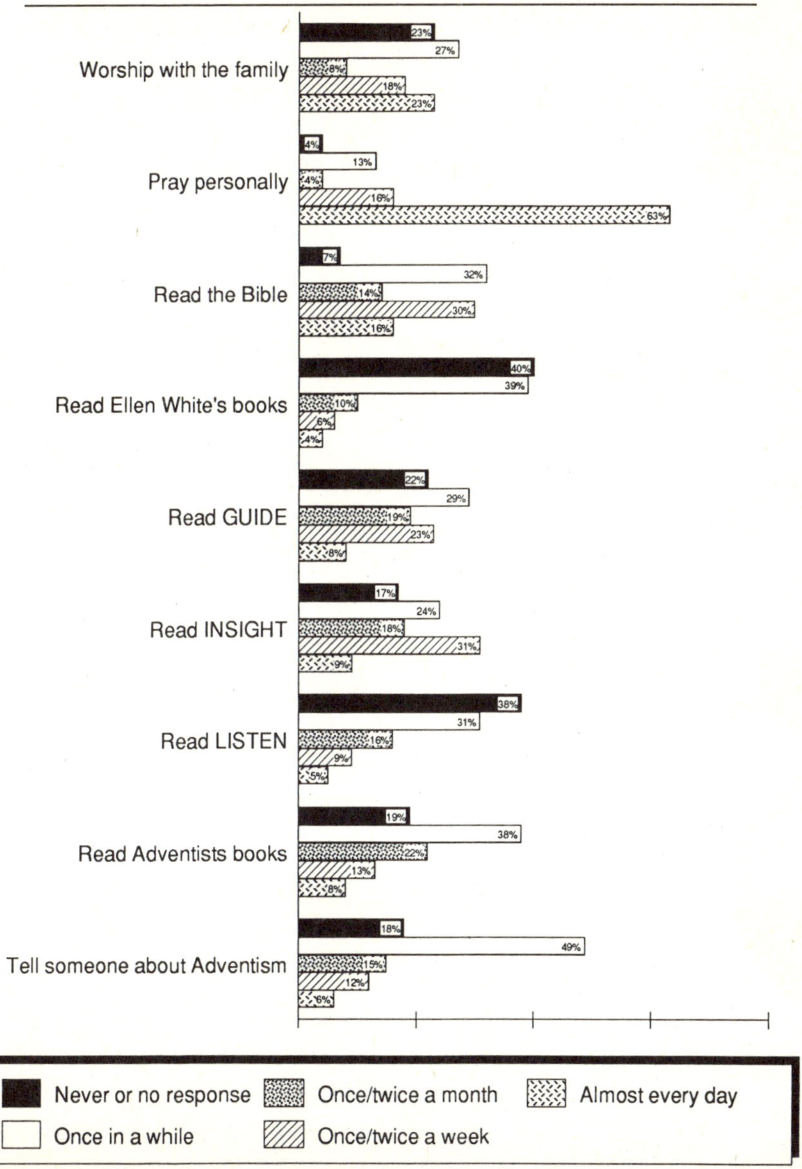

	Never or no response	Once in a while	Once/twice a month	Once/twice a week	Almost every day
Worship with the family	23%	27%	8%	18%	23%
Pray personally	4%	13%	4%	16%	63%
Read the Bible	7%	32%	14%	30%	16%
Read Ellen White's books	40%	39%	10%	6%	4%
Read GUIDE	22%	29%	19%	23%	8%
Read INSIGHT	17%	24%	18%	31%	9%
Read LISTEN	38%	31%	16%	9%	5%
Read Adventists books	19%	38%	22%	13%	8%
Tell someone about Adventism	18%	49%	15%	12%	6%

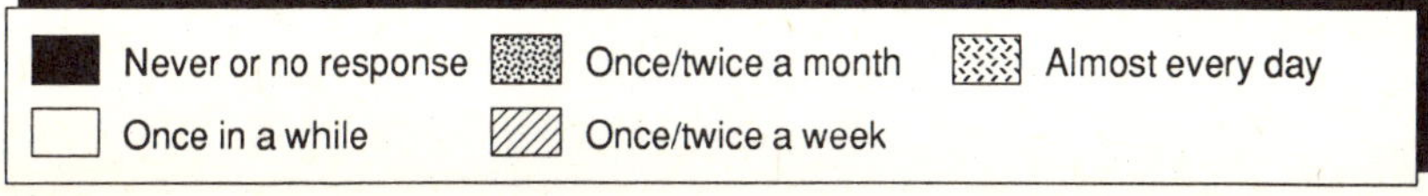

praying is worship, thanksgiving, or supplication for forgiveness for personal sins and blessings for others we cannot tell. Still, as a devotional exercise, prayer—for whatever reason—ranks far ahead of any other practice. And, as we shall see, it correlates impressively with some positive religious attitudes.

After prayer a big drop off occurs before the next behavior—reading the Bible. Only 16 percent read the Word daily, but when the next group is added, nearly half (46 percent) read at least weekly. Only 7 percent never open the covers of the Book, but a third explore the interior only "once in a while." Again, the picture may be bleaker than the figures indicate, for we can not tell how much actual "devotional reading" takes place—searching the Scriptures with the intention of facilitating spiritual growth. The youth may have included preparation of school Bible assignments, a glance at the Sabbath school quarterly, or even hearing someone else read aloud in worship.

It is evident that Adventist teenagers are not reading Ellen White to any appreciable extent. Only 20 percent claim to spend any time with her works as often as once a month. And some of this may be the result of school assignments or hearing a parent read in worship. Given the importance of Ellen White in Adventist history and theology, the church faces a real challenge to make her relevant to the contemporary generation.

It would be unrealistic to expect daily reading of the four journals listed since they are published periodically. The *Adventist Review* has a small toehold on this group, but 40 percent regularly read *Insight* regularly, and a third are still interested in *Guide*. Certainly, there is still plenty of room for improvement in marketing these journals to this target population.

Adventist books fare a bit better with close to half of the adolescents doing some reading on at least a monthly basis. However, we can't be sure that they are choosing works of a devotional nature.

Our next task is to discover what influence these devotional practices have on attitudes toward religion and the church.

The Prayer Difference

We divided the young people into three groups on the basis of their prayer frequency. The first group consisted of those who never pray or do so only once in a while. The second group contained those who pray at least once a month but not more than twice a week. The third class incorporated those who pray almost every day. For each category we calculated the percentages of those who agree strongly or agree somewhat with 12 important statements dealing with attitudes toward religion and the church. The most enlightening results of this procedure are displayed in Table 11-2.

Notice that in every single case a linear relation exists between frequency of prayer and religious attitudes. The more frequent the prayer life, the more positive the attitude toward religion and the church. For most items this means that the percentages rise as the frequency of prayer increases. But for the two negatively worded items—"I feel rebellious toward my religion" and "Good Adventists have less fun than other people"—the positive calls for *disagreement*, and thus the percentages decline as the youth pray more frequently.

Not only are all 36 figures in the "expected" direction, if prayer does indeed influence attitudes, but in most cases the differences between them are substantial. With the exception of three differences, they are all 10 or more points apart and reach as much as 28 points. Of the three exceptions, two are 9 points apart. The only nonsignificant difference (2 points) occurs between those who pray rarely and those who pray spasmodically on the statement, "Good Adventists have less fun than other people."

Large differences occur in important areas. We consider the item "I intend to remain an active Adventist when I am on my own" to be the *key statement* on the questionnaire for our purposes. Here 22 points separate the nonpraying youth from the occasional supplicators and another 20 points divide the latter

TABLE 11-2

Relationship of RELIGIOUS ATTITUDES AND FREQUENCY OF PRAYER

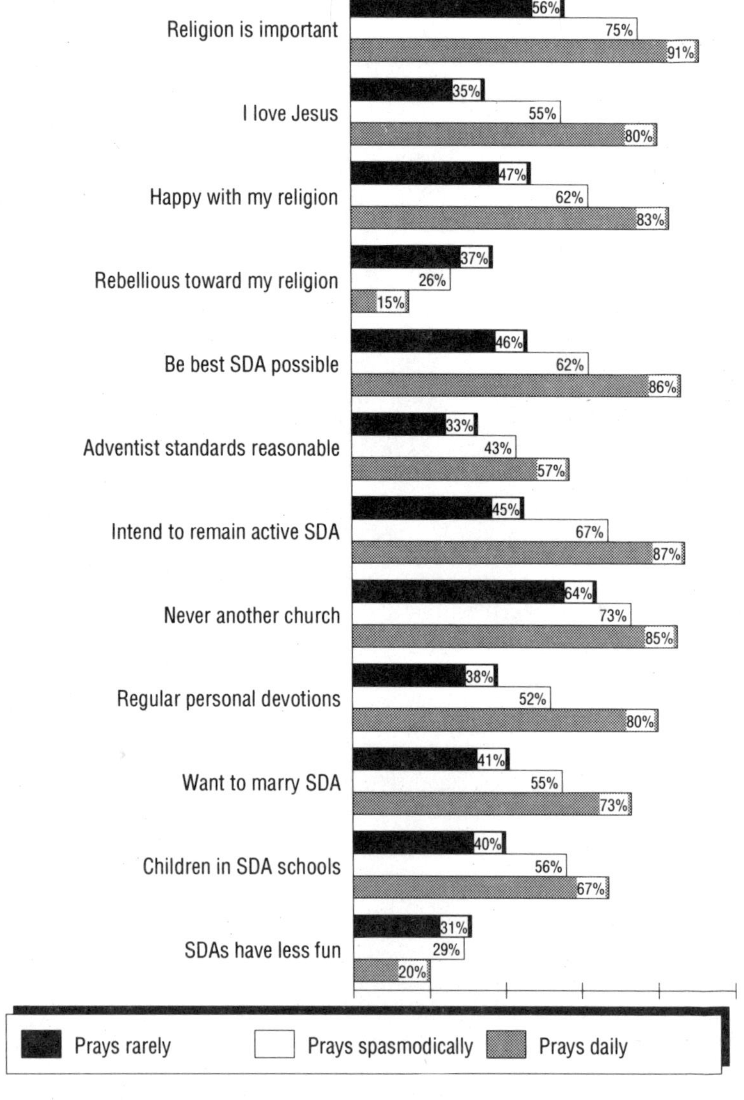

from those who pray daily. You may recall from the list given in chapter 10 that frequency of personal prayer was the *second-ranked* of 12 variables that significantly predicted intention to remain an Adventist. Indeed, as Table 11-2 reveals, 87 percent of those who pray daily intend to remain in the church. So important is regular personal prayer that only agreement with Adventist standards exceeds it as a predictor of youth retention.

Notable spreads are also found for "Religion is important in my life," "I have a love experience with Jesus Christ," "I want to be the best Adventist Christian I can possibly be," and "I want to have personal devotions regularly when I am on my own."

Frequency of prayer predicts religious attitudes to a remarkable degree.

The Bible-reading Difference

We also divided our adolescents into three groups based on their frequency of reading the Bible. These are (1) those who read the Bible once in a while or never, (2) those who read the Bible at least monthly but not more than twice a week, and (3) those who read the Bible almost every day. Of course, the composition of these groups is not the same as for the frequency-of-prayer classifications, since far fewer young people reported reading the Bible on a daily basis than they did praying. Again, we calculated the percentages in each group who agreed with the same 12 key statements shown above. The results are displayed in Table 11-3.

The pattern is similar to that for prayer. Every single case shows a linear progression with those reading the Bible more frequently having more positive attitudes toward religion and the church. As before, the differences tend to be substantial and significant. The smallest spread is 5 points, and there are only two differences in that range. The spread reaches 28 points in one case.

An interesting observation is that the larger differences tend to occur between the first two groups, with smaller spreads between groups two and three. This is partly explained by the fact

TABLE 11-3

Relationship of RELIGIOUS ATTITUDES AND FREQUENCY OF BIBLE READING

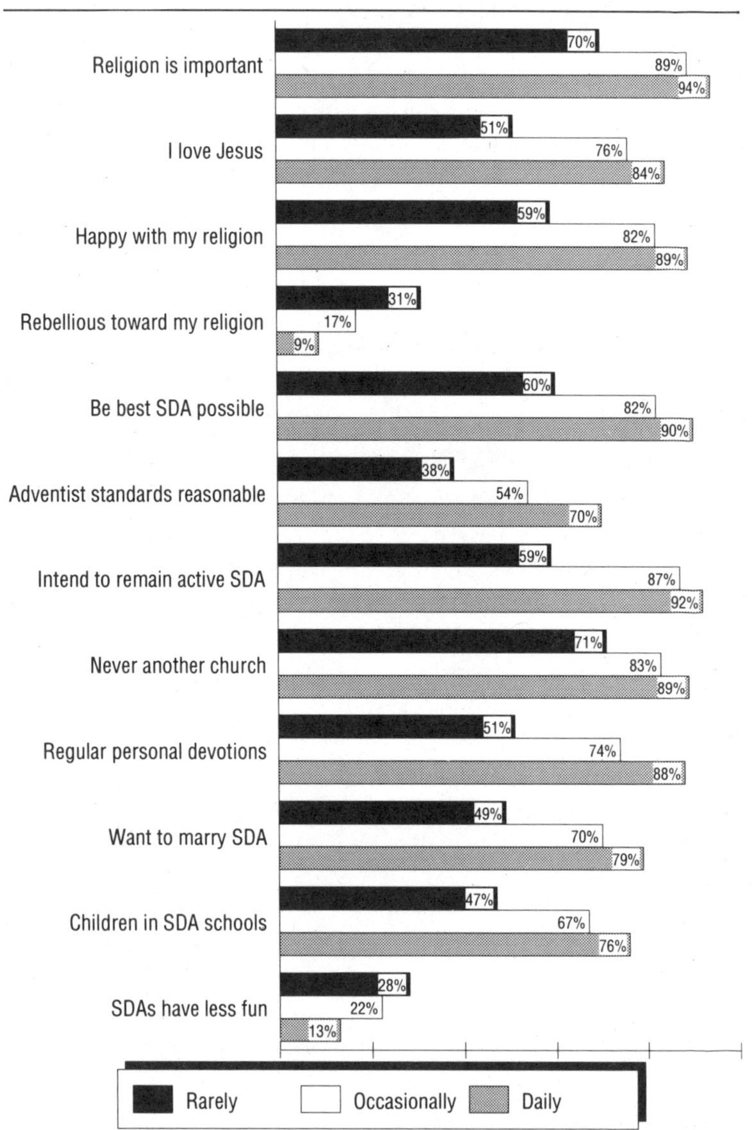

that agreement tends to be quite high for the occasional readers, leaving a smaller area for expansion by the daily readers.

Again, prominent differences surface on the key question—"I intend to remain an active Adventist when I am on my own"—with 28 points separating the first two groups and another 5 points between groups two and three. In all, at least 30 percentage points lie between group one (nonreaders) and group three (daily readers) on 8 of the 12 items and at least 20 points on two others.

Frequency of Bible reading proved to be the ninth-ranked predictor of the 27 items (12 of which were found to be statistically significant) employed in a multiple correlation with "intention to remain in the Adventist Church" (see list in chapter 10). Table 11-3 reveals that a whopping 92 percent of those who report daily Bible reading also plan to remain in the church.

The Spirit of Prophecy Difference

As a final comparison we looked at differences based on the frequency of reading Ellen White's books. Because *daily* reading (unlike prayer and Bible study) seemed more than could be expected, we divided our sample here into only two groups. The first group consists of those who read Ellen White only once in a while or never. We can call them the nonreaders. The second group contains those who read her books at least once a month and probably more often. These are the readers. Nonreaders outnumber readers four to one. We calculated the percentages in each group who agreed with the same 12 key statements shown above. The results are displayed in Table 11-4.

In every case the readers are more positive toward religion and the church than are the nonreaders. The differences are substantial, ranging from 8 to 25 percentage points. Especially dramatic are the differences in believing Adventist rules and standards to be reasonable, wanting to have personal devotions when on their own, and desiring for their children to have an Adventist education.

TABLE 11-4

Relationship of
RELIGIOUS ATTITUDES AND READING OF ELLEN G. WHITE

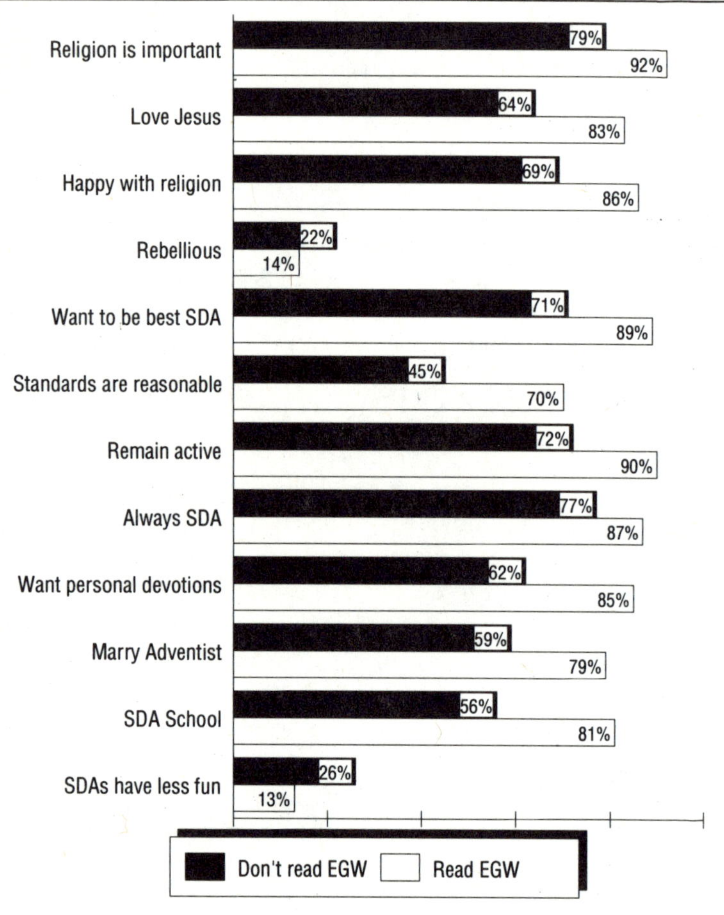

When we recall that the extent of agreement with Adventist standards/rules was the number one predictor of intention to remain Adventists, and find on Table 11-4 that 25 percent more Ellen White readers than nonreaders felt positive toward those standards, it seems critical that the youth be exposed to the principles behind the standards as found in the counsel given by Ellen White.

Do Devotions Make a Difference?

We have selected three measures of devotional behavior. When we related these measures to key statements of attitudes toward religion and the church, we found that the more frequent the devotion, the more positive the attitude. This finding held for all three measures on all 12 statements; *in not one instance* was there a reversal of the pattern. The statistical probability of this happening by chance is so low as to be virtually impossible. The relationship is real and strong.

This is not to say that praying, reading the Bible, or spending time with Ellen White will automatically cause a teenager to feel positive about religion and to remain in the church. Perhaps those individuals who are religiously positive tend naturally to seek devotional aids to strengthen their Christian experience. Perhaps some third factor is influencing both attitudes and devotional behavior. Nevertheless, the relationship is present. Most likely, the effect is circular with both factors stimulating each other.

From a practical standpoint, that seems to say that adolescents will probably not love the church or remain in it unless they have a strong devotional life. This offers hope, because we can break into the cycle at any point. The relationship should challenge us to find ways to make prayer, Bible study, and the counsels of Ellen White fresh, relevant, and exciting to the rising generation.

References

*David Wilkerson, *Hey Preach—You're Comin' Through!* (Old Tappan, NJ: Fleming H. Revell Company, 1968), pp. 13-15.

CHAPTER 12

One Year Later

We started out to write a book about what we had learned about Adventist teenagers during the first year of our 10-year study. But while we have been struggling to analyze, organize, and make sense out of our massive data bank of 150 bits of information on over 1500 young people, time has slipped by. We have now surveyed our sample for the second year. Since we have this latest information in hand, we decided to include a final chapter on the second stage of the study so that our readers could see not only the state of things at the beginning but also the direction in which they are going.

In the first place **Adventist Youth Survey 2** was considerably shorter than its predecessor; it contained only 17 questions on two pages. We believed that after asking the youth to complete the complex and time-consuming survey of the first year, we needed to come back with something easy that would encourage them to stay with the study. The period between the first and second years is a particularly crucial one because first-year respondents have not yet made an ongoing commitment to the research. If we could entice them to participate a second time, they might begin to experience a relationship with us that would encourage them to respond in subsequent years.

Part of maintaining this relationship is to keep track of any residential changes. People today are highly mobile, and after a year the postal system will no longer forward mail. So the very first question we asked was: "Is the address on the envelope in which we mailed this questionnaire still your correct one?" Those answering "no" were instructed to fill in the correct address in the blank space provided.

We had expected that some attrition would occur. Indeed, this was why we began with such a large sample; we wanted to be sure we would still have a group sufficiently large for appropriate analyses at the end of 10 years. We mailed the survey to 1,523 young people (see appendix), and after two follow-up mailings we secured 1,263 usable instruments—an 83 percent response rate. At the time of the data collection, these adolescents were all 16 or 17 years old. Here is what has been happening to them.

Personal Religion

We asked an especially pertinent question: "How does your present relationship with Jesus Christ compare with that of one year ago?"

They answered:

Stronger today	32%
About the same	45%
Weaker today	21%
Have no relationship	2%

We can find encouragement in the fact that growth is greater than decline and that more than three-fourths have either held their own or gained in their spiritual experience. But we also should be disturbed that nearly a fourth are either slipping in their religious lives or have given up the battle altogether.

Obviously, religious experience is sustained by the devotional life. So we asked how often these teenagers engaged in three faith-building practices. They could rate themselves from 1 to 4 with 1 being "seldom or never" and 4 being "daily."

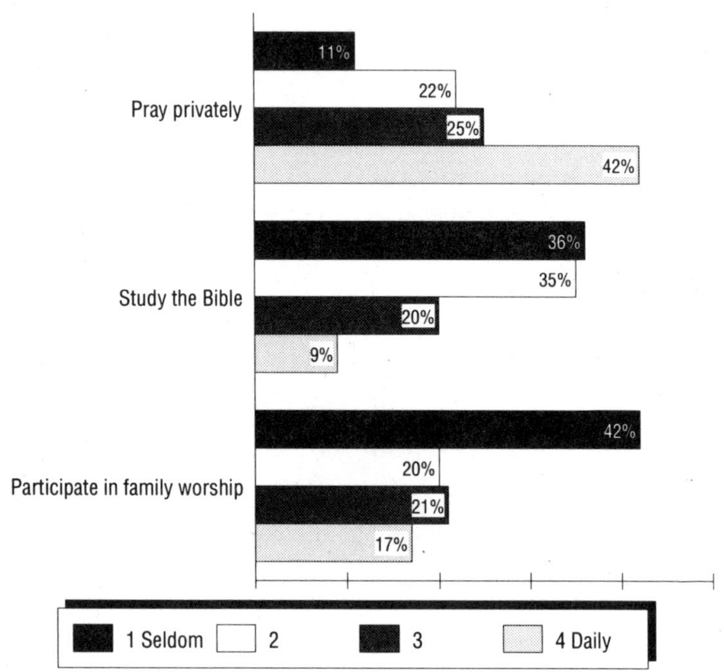

While only a minority are praying privately on a daily basis, *personal prayer* still outranks any other devotional practice, and nearly 90 percent pray at least occasionally. *Bible study* fares poorly with less than a tenth reading the Scriptures devotionally every day and more than a third never spending personal time with the Word. *Family worship* also shows up to be nonexistent or only sporadic with the great majority.

It seems that the church must seek ways to make personal Bible study meaningful and satisfying to adolescents and to encourage family worship in the homes. Without a change here, much more slippage in spiritual vitality may be expected in the coming years.

The Family Context

From the first-year data, we have already discovered the significant influence of family variables on the religious life of the teenager. So we asked about some possible crisis events during the past 12 months. "Have any of the following happened in your family during the last year?"

	Yes	No
Your parents separated or divorced	6%	94%
One or both parents died	1%	99%
One or both parents left the church	8%	92%

Only small percentages experienced any of these tragedies. Still, in just one year, 79 of our teenagers saw their homes broken up by marital discord, 17 lost parents through death, and 105 felt what must have been a faith-wrenching experience when one or both of their parents left the church. Crises like these have to be discouraging to one's Christian walk.

And, indeed, they do make a difference. For example, on the question as to how their present relationship with Jesus Christ compares with that of a year ago, 25 percent of those whose parents had divorced said "stronger," and 38 percent said "weaker." For those whose homes had not been split, the figures were 32 percent and 20 percent. The 18 percent differential on the weakening of the spiritual life is especially disturbing.

When the question concerned relationship with the church during the past year, 33 percent of the group whose parents had divorced said it was weaker compared to 23 percent of the group who had not experienced this disruption. And 8 percent of the former group no longer relate to the church compared with 4 percent of the latter—double the tragedy.

Youth from those homes that did not break up in the preceding year are much better church attenders too—66 percent go every week, and only 8 percent never attend. But of those suffering the trauma of divorce only half go weekly, and 17 percent never attend. Divorce not only brings personal pain to the family members, but it also seems to affect adversely the spiritual experience of the children.

Apparently, divorce not only separates husbands and wives but also parents and children. Of those teenagers whose parents recently divorced, 32 percent say they are farther apart from their fathers, and 28 percent say they are farther apart from their mothers today. For the other group, the figures are only 12 percent and 12 percent. And in 46 percent of the homes that experienced divorce, one or both parents left the church during the past year—indicating how closely spiritual values can be intertwined with family values. In contrast, a parent left the church in only 6 percent of the homes where divorce did not occur.

The negative effects of divorce may be summed up in a chart comparing those who answered "yes" and "no" to the question: Did your parents become separated or divorced in the last year?

	Yes	No
Relationship with Jesus weaker	38%	20%
Relationship with church weaker	33%	23%
Regular church attenders	50%	66%
Farther apart from father	32%	12%
Farther apart from mother	28%	12%

From this relationship, we might infer that having parents drop out of the church would have a negative relationship upon the spiritual life of the teenagers—and we would be correct. In homes where a parent recently apostatized, 32 percent of the youth say that their relationship with Jesus Christ is weaker than a year ago, and 48 percent report their relationship with the Adventist Church is weaker. For homes that did not suffer this spiritual disruption the comparable figures are 20 percent and 21 percent.

Where parents did not disaffiliate in the past year, 68 percent of the youth attend church at least weekly. But where one or both parents dropped membership, only 35 percent do so. And 36 percent of those whose parents did not leave the fold hold an office or other service position in the church in contrast to 22 percent of the teenagers whose parents dropped out.

Finally, of the adolescents whose parents left the church, 27 percent have a more distant relationship with their mothers and 28 percent a more distant relationship with their fathers than they did a year previously. For those whose parents remained in the church, the comparable figures are 11 percent and 12 percent.

If we could only get parents to be faithful, both to the church and to each other, many of the spiritual problems with our youth might never occur.

Another chart may summarize the comparisons between those who answered "yes" and "no" to the question: Did one or both of your parents leave the church during this last year?

	Yes	No
Relationship with Jesus weaker	32%	20%
Relationship with church weaker	48%	21%
Regular church attenders	35%	68%
Hold a church office	22%	36%
Farther apart from father	28%	12%
Farther apart from mother	27%	11%

Throughout this study we have continually stressed the importance of relationships. Given the keystone position of parent-child interaction, we asked: "How does the closeness of your relationship with your mother compare with that of a year ago?" Our sample answered as followed:

Farther apart today	13%
About the same	46%
Closer today	40%
Not applicable	1%

Since adolescence is a turbulent time, which is usually filled with stress and conflict between young people trying to assert their independence and parents trying to preserve their authority, to find 40 percent of these mid-teenagers growing closer to their mothers is a real sign of hope.

The same question for fathers yielded these results:

Farther apart today	13%
About the same	49%
Closer today	30%
Not applicable	8%

While the same percentages are farther apart from both mother and father than they were a year previously, not as many have grown closer to the father as have to the mother during that time. However, the major share of the discrepancy can be attributed to the "not applicable" category. This probably suggests absent fathers (through divorce or death) to which the youth cannot relate at all—either positively or negatively.

Connection to the Church

The main purpose of the study is to investigate the retention in or dropping out from the church. So we asked several questions about attitudes toward the church and participation in its life. Perhaps most important was: "How does your present relationship with the Seventh-day Adventist Church compare with that of one year ago?" Here is what we found:

Stronger today	23%
About the same	50%
Weaker today	23%
No longer relate to the church	4%

So half of the sample hasn't changed over the past year; of the remainder, those who have grown closer and those who have become more distant are about equally divided; and a small percentage have already given up on the church.

In the first-year data, attitudes toward Adventist standards or rules were the leading predictors of whether or not the teenagers intended to remain in the church when they were on their own. So we came back to that theme: "How do you feel about the lifestyle standards of the Adventist Church (music, sex, recreation, health, dress, et cetera)?"

Mostly agree	37%
Mixed feelings	54%
Mostly disagree	9%

Fewer than 10 percent are totally out of harmony with Adventist lifestyle. But more than half have mixed feelings. Given the results from the first year, we interpret these mixed feelings not as general ambivalence toward the standards but as meaning that the youth agree with some and disagree with others. This would be in line with what we reported in a previous chapter and would indicate that things have not changed much.

How often do these young people attend church (if they are

not forced to)? About two-thirds are regular attenders, and fewer than 10 percent do not go at all. The breakdown looks like this:

Rarely or never	9%
Once every month or two	6%
Two or three times a month	20%
At least once a week	65%

Is their religious activity confined to merely putting in an appearance though? How active in the life of the church are they after they get there? About 35 percent said they hold an office or other service position in their local congregations; the other 65 percent do not. We need to find ways to tie teenagers more closely into the structure of the organized church.

We also asked how active they had been during the past year in outreach or witnessing activities. This is what they told us:

Rarely or never	57%
At least six times a year	22%
At least once a month	15%
At least once a week	6%

It appears that about a fifth are quite regular in outreach activities. One of the greatest challenges to denominational youth leaders today is to find ways to involve the majority who are not active in the church, although many of them attend regularly.

Pouring Out the Heart

While most of our questions were forced-choice, we gave one opportunity for the respondents to pour out their hearts: "Is there anything else you would like to say about your relationship with the Adventist Church?"

More than half (54 percent) chose not to respond. The others wrote in opinions, which we have tried to classify into logical groupings. We have identified 703 comments, with some youth providing items for more than one classification. Numbers in parentheses are head counts.

The largest category (225) addressed the church directly. Of these, one group (58) talked about their happiness with the church and what it meant to them. A nearly equal-sized group lamented that the church does not relate to teens or meet their needs. Others (41) believe that the church is too legalistic with its nitpicking rules. Some (20), however, worried that the church was becoming too liberal and needed to raise its standards. Then there were those (33) who felt that the church was lifeless, cold, and boring and needed more excitement. A few (6) even implored the church to do everything possible to save its youth—the future of the church.

The youth in the second largest main category (197) wrote about their spiritual lives. Many (52) expressed the desire to come closer to Christ—to grow spiritually. Others (31) gave a glowing report of their Christian progress—their spiritual experience has been growing stronger, and religion is becoming more real to them. About equal numbers spoke positively (45) of their love for their faith and their happiness with their religion and negatively (47) about their discouragement with their Christian walk.

A third main category of responses (88) concerned the leaders and members of the church. Much of this was negative (73), citing problems in the church like gossiping, hypocrisy, unfriendliness, holier-than-thou attitudes, and politics. But a few (6) talked about a special leader whom they liked and trusted. Some (6) even complained about the frequent transfers of pastors and getting "left-over ministers."

Another group (65) spoke to the social life of the church. Most of these (43) cried out for more youth activities or complained of no youth their own age in the congregation (7). A few (4) wrote about the difficulty of peer pressure or relationships with parents (4). But several (5) took time to praise parents for the support they are providing the youth.

Some youth (30) wrote about the educational system. These divided into those who were hostile toward Adventist schools (8) and didn't want to attend them and those who extolled the benefits of Adventist academies (22).

Among the other miscellaneous comments, seven criticized Sabbath sermons, three praised them, five were negative about Ellen White, and eight requested personal prayer for themselves. Believe it or not—12 even expressed appreciation for the survey.

Plans for the Future

As our teenagers filled out this survey in the summer of 1988 (a small percentage of returns came in through the autumn months), what were their plans for the future? Where did they see themselves attending during the 1988-89 school year? Here is what they told us:

Adventist academy	47%
Public high school	35%
Home study courses	2%
College	9%
Not in school	2%
Other plan	5%

The results of the first-year survey had shown that about half (51 percent) of the teenagers were in Adventist academies, and this pattern probably has changed little if we can assume that the 9 percent going to college is also divided roughly equally between Adventist and non-Adventist institutions. In the next few years, we will be analyzing the college scene as our sample passes out of the secondary-school period.

For now, we continue to watch and to listen. We continue to note the positive trends that cheer our hearts and the disturbing signs that trouble our serenity. We continue to call for the church to make use of this material to discern the dangers and to intervene to meet them. We would not be simply recorders of the process by which our youth march out of the church in droves. We would be change agents.

We pray that because of this ongoing study, and its frequent reports, the history of Adventist youth will turn out differently than if this research had never been conducted. But to change these foreshadowings will take all of us—working together under the direction of the divine Youth Ministry Professional.

Afterword

Boarding academy is so unrealistic that by the time we graduate and move out into the real world, the shock either makes us stay in the SDA system or drop the church completely. Since I have graduated, I have not attended church, and neither have any of my friends. It's been almost four years since you started this survey. I don't see that it's done any good. I mean, isn't there any hope for our SDA youth? We're the future. Sooner or later you guys are going to die. What then?''

What then indeed? Young people at risk to the church. And yet, youth wanting to see the church become meaningful in their lives. And the tottering future of Adventism. All these themes emerge in the ambivalent responses of our sample as we continue to collect our data—now in the third year.

From June to December of 1989 we have been working hard to collect responses to our third annual survey. As this book goes to press, we have not finished collecting, nor have we begun to analyze the data. But as a brief postscript, we can give some preliminary information on the first 1,000 teenagers to respond. This will provide the reader with some idea of how this study is continuing to develop.

Our teenagers are now all 17 or 18 years of age. While all were in secondary schools at the beginning of the study, 39 percent have now graduated and moved on—15 percent to

Adventist colleges, 15 percent to non-Adventist colleges, and the remaining 9 percent to work or other pursuits. Twenty-two of them (2 percent) have married already, with another 5 percent engaged, but the remaining 93 percent are still single with no definite plans. About two thirds have decided on a lifetime occupation.

Are they starting to leave the church? Yes. Of the first 1,003 replies, 50 (5 percent) have indicated that they have dropped out. In addition, some of those who haven't replied this year may be dropouts who are simply not responding. Those who have written have described their current relationship with the church as follows:

Enthusiastic member	24%
So-so member	52%
Officially a member, but not in heart	19%
Have dropped out (50 youth)	5%

Notice that not only have we definitely lost 50 young people to the church, but nearly four times that number no longer consider themselves Adventists even though their names are still registered on the books of some congregation.

Since one of the prime goals of the 10-year study is to probe reasons that youth leave the church, we have constructed a special questionnaire that we have sent to each of the 50 dropouts and that we intend to send to each person in the future who leaves the church. It explores the strength of various factors in the decision to leave, feelings at the time of leaving, and the extent to which the congregation tried to intervene to prevent the loss or has worked to restore the dropout. It asks what might have been different and would have prevented this tragedy. It also inquires as to the likelihood of the youth returning to the faith in the future. As these data accumulate, we will be issuing reports to the church in North America.

It's one thing to be in the church; it's another thing to be active. Here is how our sample saw their level of activity:

Very active	10%
Reasonably active	27%
Only occasionally	37%
Never do anything	26%

If involvement in the life of the congregation is a key to retaining our youth, it has to be disconcerting to note that nearly two thirds (63 percent) are essentially dormant. But maybe we don't invite them to participate. Maybe they don't feel welcome. We asked our group how important they thought they were to their local Adventist church at the present time. The results?

Vital to their program	10%
Somewhat necessary	58%
They don't know I exist	32%

How sad is the condition of the third in the last group. Only a tenth sense that the church depends on them. And nearly half the sample (45 percent) declared that their local church had no youth program events or provided no youth ministry other than Sabbath school.

Retention is based not only on activity, however, but on spirituality. What is happening in their personal religious experiences as the years roll by?

Present relationship with Jesus Christ compared with two years ago	
Strong today	31%
About the same	38%
Weaker today	28%
No relation	3%

Here we seem to be losing at almost the same rate we are gaining. Like most of the results of this survey, both encouraging and ominous themes emerge.

Any more bad news? Well, about a third say that more than half the young people in their age group with whom they are acquainted use alcohol on more than just an experimental basis. And nearly 10 percent say the same thing about illegal drugs. Furthermore, two thirds of the sample estimate that less than half their acquaintances are still virgins. Of course, some of these "friends" may not be Adventists, but certainly some of them are. Alcohol, drugs, and premarital sex threaten to torpedo the relationship of our youth with Christ and His church. We have hardly begun to meet this challenge.

Is there any *good* news? We asked our sample if they would be interested in participating in a variety of novel witnessing experiences. They could decline outright, indicate some interest, or say they would be very interested. If we combine the last two categories, we have the following percentages of those who have some or much interest in participating in the following experiences:

One-day youth discipleship seminar	88%
Short-term mission project	89%
Community service project	88%
Youth-to-youth seminar for drug-free youth	87%
Sending youth missionary magazine to non-Adventist friend	82%
Wilderness experience like Outward Bound	82%

It seems remarkable that in spite of the moderate level of spirituality and current church activity, overwhelming numbers of our sample exhibit at least some interest in creative ventures for Christ. Our youth seem to be saying: "I may not be a great Adventist right now, but I really would like to get involved if you could challenge me with amission worth an investment of my life."

While it is not central to our study, in view of the current struggle within the church over the role of women in the ministry, we asked our sample if qualified women should be ordained to the pastoral ministry. The majority (59 percent) said yes. Another 28 percent were uncertain, and only 13 percent disagreed. If these youth remain within the church and do not become more conservative as they age, the next generation may handle the problem differently than the present one has.

And these youth are not politically liberal. If they had been of voting age in 1988, half would have voted for George Bush, only 20 percent for Michael Dukakis, and the final 30 percent would not have voted.

How shall we sum up all these conflicting findings? We are convinced that while our youth are at risk to Christ and His church, the lives of caring and loving parents, pastors, teachers, and other adults can make a difference. Hear this message from one of our young women who writes to us and to the church.

"When I first started this survey, I was very rebellious, with an attitude that whatever the school or church said I shouldn't do, I wanted to do. Fortunately, I was always in an environment where God was first. At school the constant reminder of God and His love broke down my defenses. All I can say is that being surrounded by people who focused more on God's love and forgiveness and not so much on the rules and regulations that people have set changed me.

"As a result of the love that was taught to me, I no longer have the urge to break the rules of the church and school. Concentrate on teaching love as Jesus did, rather than rules and standards. Love will eventually win anyone. Thanks for listening. Much love and prayers."

Appendix

Methodology of the Study

It seems appropriate to supply some detail as to the methods we used to locate and survey more than 1,500 Adventist teenagers. Since many readers will want only the results and will not much care *how* we obtained them, we have put this material in an appendix rather than allowing it to impede the flow of the regular text. For those who are interested in such details or for those who would like to check up on the soundness of our practice, we felt it would be essential to include some such statement.

Selecting the Sample

The population for this study was the 15- and 16-year-old baptized membership of the Seventh-day Adventist Church in the North American Division. Included were youth in Adventist schools, in other schools, and those not attending school.

We began by selecting sample churches. From lists of the churches in each conference, we selected one church for each 1,000 members or major fraction thereof in the conference, using a computer random-selection program. This yielded 695 churches. We wrote to the clerk of each church and requested names and addresses of all youth on the membership records who were either 15 or 16 years old. Cooperation was not gained without some hard work, but after six months, three letters of appeal, and scores of phone calls, we received lists from 659 clerks—a 95 percent response rate.

Research Instrument

In the meantime we were designing the questionnaire. This was a lengthy process that involved obtaining critiques from division leaders, youth-ministry workers, and measurement professionals. It also included a pilot test with 20 target-age youth who were members of a single congregation. After a number of revisions, the final instrument was six pages long and collected approximately 150 separate items of information. Many of the items utilized a five-point, Likert-type scale to rate various statements (strongly agree to strongly disagree, most helpful to most unhelpful, et cetera). Other questions were in multiple-choice format. The instrument concluded with five open-ended statements.

Data Collection

The lists from the clerks generated 2,639 good addresses (plus 111 letters returned as undeliverable). Three separate mailings were sent to the teenagers on these lists over a seven-month period. Each mailing included not only a questionnaire but a letter of entreaty and a stamped return envelope.

After seven months we had responses from 1,676 teenagers (63.5 percent), but 165 proved to be either not church members or in the wrong age group. So the final group on which the study was conducted totaled 1,511 Adventist youth of 15 or 16 years old.

After the cut-off date for data analysis had passed, 12 more usable questionnaires were received. While these youth will be followed up as part of the longitudinal study, except for a few instances, their responses have not been included in the data analyses on which this book is based.

Statistical Analyses

The responses were entered into a computer and tallied so that the percentage choosing each possible response on each question was displayed. By using a cross-tabulations program, we developed a series of profiles that revealed how various subgroups responded to the items. Subgroup differences are discussed at length throughout the chapters of the book. We also categorized the answers from the five free-response questions into 41 areas and compared them with the quantitative data derived from the other questions.

The major statistical method for examining the data was by Pearson correlation coefficients. Correlations were determined between the attitudes and behaviors measured by the instrument and the various family, church, and school background variables reported. In some cases variables were compared by the *t*-test for independent means. A multiple-regression analysis was performed on the dependent variable "intention to remain an Adventist" to identify in descending order the strength of all the separate influences on the teenagers' attitudes toward church retention or attrition.

While these procedures have provided the information that undergirds our report, in the actual writing of the chapters we have kept the lay reader in mind and have not used technical statistical language. We have chosen to set forth our findings in a straightforward manner that will be clear and sensible to the reader who is not schooled in formal statistics. Those readers who wish a more complete description of the methodology may refer to Janet Leigh Kangas, "A Study of the Religious Attitudes and Behaviors of Seventh-day Adventist Adolescents in North America Related to Their Family, Educational, and Church Backgrounds" (Ph.D. dissertation, Andrews University, 1988), pages 66-79.

This process then provided our ''ears'' for listening to teenage concerns. The young people wrote openly and frankly. Some of the material was humorous; some heartbreaking. All of it will be useful to the church in planning youth ministry.